A PRACTICAL APPROACH TO THE STUDY OF INDIAN CAPITAL MARKETS

A PRACTICAL APPROACH TO THE STUDY OF INDIAN CAPITAL MARKETS

G S Ramachandra;
Kuldeep Dongre

PARTRIDGE
A Penguin Random House Company

ISBN: Softcover   978-1-4828-5751-1
                 eBook   978-1-4828-5752-8

Print information available on the last page.

To order additional copies of this book, contact
Partridge India
000 800 10062 62
orders.india@partridgepublishing.com

www.partridgepublishing.com/india

Table of Contents

FOREWORD

Today, India stands tallest among the capital markets. It has a long history of about 150 years. Since 1992, with the globalization the Indian capital market has developed in leaps and bounds. Capital markets play a pivotal role in capital supply which is the life-blood of any economy. It is now a huge opportunity for both learners and investors to be actively involved in the process of nation building. Capital market is not all that easy to be understood by an average investor. A number of books as well as monographs have already been published to help learners enter the capital market. However, it could do with building some additional awareness around this topic.

This book serves as a vehicle to introduce you to the fundamentals of Indian Capital Markets. An effort is made to simplify the concepts and present it in such a way that the concepts are clearly understood even by a novice. In modern times, financial literacy is just as important as any other discipline. Every individual needs to understand the fundamentals of finance and economics and how it helps in the development process of an economy.

We have attempted to share our combined 3 decade worth of experience in capital markets in a simple and instructive manner covering both theoretical and practical aspects of the capital market. Being successful in Indian capital markets requires a sound understanding of first principles, discipline in investing and loads of patience!

We have consulted a number of authorities, books and resources on the internet to design the content of this book. Special thanks to Prof. B. Deenadas Shetty, Prof. K. Krishnamurthy, Prof. B. Sadashiva Rao and Mr. Alok Agarwal for reading the manuscript and providing valuable feedback. We hope the readers find this useful.

G. S. Ramachandra

Kuldeep Dongre

CHAPTER I

A Typical Business Case[1]

Ram is a retail merchant in a town. He has a flourishing retail business with approximate annual revenue of **Rs.20 lacs**. His gross-profit from the business is close to about **30%** which means that he makes a gross annual profit of about **Rs.6 lacs.** For a while now, Ram has been thinking about expanding his business as he sees lot of potential to expand the business in nearby towns. His estimate is about **Rs.12 lacs** to set up an additional retail outlet. He approaches banks to raise the required capital. Ram is not very happy with the high interest rates of the loans the banks have to offer and hence decides not to go for a loan. Fortunately, at the same time, an investor named Sundar arrives in town and is looking for good opportunity to invest. Through a common friend, Sundar meets Ram and proposes to invest in his business and help Ram to expand. Ram now has a partner who is willing to invest in his business which will help him realize his dream

---

[1] This is a fictitious business and all the characters of the business case are fictitious

of expanding his business. Sundar, on the other hand is happy to invest because he knows that the business that Ram owns is profitable and will yield good returns in the long run. Ram and Sundar are now partners in the business.

A few years pass by. Ram's business now is known as **"Retail Enterprises[2]"**, has **4 partners** and **12 retail outlets** in **12 different** towns. The business generates annual revenue of **Rs.5 crore** with a gross profit margin of **40%** which amounts to an annual gross margin of **Rs.2 crore**.

Ram and his 4 business partners are now working on a grand business expansion plan of setting about **200 outlets** in key cities in India in addition to an online business which will involve setting up of a website that will facilitate online selling and delivery of goods to customers. The approximate funding required to expand this business stands at about **Rs.100 crores.**

Rs.100 crore being a fairly large sum of money needs to be funded from a number of investors and banks. This is where the role of capital markets comes into picture. The subsequent chapters will delve into details of Indian Capital Markets.

---

[2] This is a fictitious company.

CHAPTER II

Funding Sources – Concept Of Debt And Equity

One may now ask as to what are the options to fund the setting up of *"Retail Enterprises"* across 200 outlets with a fully functional online enabled platform? Several options exist to raise the funds. A few important are detailed below:

1. **VENTURE CAPITALISTS: Owners'** of *Retail Enterprises* can approach **VC**'s (venture capitalists) OR **HNI**'s (High Net-worth Individuals) OR **Private Equity firms** (PE firms) who can come together and invest a huge sum of money of **Rs.100 crores.** The **HNIs, VCs** or the **Private Equity firms** will then be partners of the business with a typical short term (5-10 years) interest in the business looking to sell off their stake in the business in the short term (5-10 years). These kind of investments are known as **equity**

investments and the investors are stakeholders or Owners of the business, extent being proportional to the money invested.

2. **LONG-TERM FINANCING: Owners'** of *Retail Enterprises* can approach multiple banks that can fund the **Rs.100 crores** through long term financing (business loans) options. The banks are then called the **creditors** to the company. Typically, loans are called debt instruments. A tailor made securitized long term financing proposal is extended by the bank after a process of close examination of the company's (Retail Enterprises) performance over the years, the profitability and the future growth potential of the enterprise. These loans are called securitized loans as it is based on mortgage receivables.

3. **COMPANY DEPOSITS: Owners'** of *Retail Enterprises* can come up with a **company deposit** (CD) instrument and open it up for all investors. Company deposits (CD) are typical debt instruments which promise a certain % annual return (typically higher than the bank deposit interest rates) and a fixed lock-in period before which it can be redeemed. Company deposit instruments need specific authorizations and need to adhere to certain guidelines issued by RBI (**R**eserve **B**ank of India). CD's can be issued by NBFC (Non-Banking Financial Companies).

4. **Initial Public Offer (IPO): Owners'** of *Retail Enterprises* can issue shares of the company which indicate part ownership of the company

to the public. The entire process of issuing shares and getting it listed as a public company is regulated by the **SEBI** (Securities Exchange Board of India). This process of issuing shares and getting listed as a public company is called **IPO**. Issuing shares is an equity instrument and provides part-ownership of the company to the equity holder. We will discuss the processes in detail in subsequent chapters.

Defining Debt and Equity

Debt instruments are issued by the issuers for borrowing monies from the investors with a defined tenure and mutually agreed terms and conditions for payment of interest and repayment of principal. Examples of debt instruments are

- ✓ *Long-term debt instruments (typically with a maturity term of more than a year)*
    - Company Deposits Or Certificates of Deposit (CDs)
    - Govt. of India issued certificates (GoI bonds/ securities)
- ✓ *Short-term debt instruments[3] (typically with a maturity term of less than a year)*
    - Commercial Paper (CPs)
    - Treasury Bills (T-Bills)

---

[3] These are also called money market instruments as they are short term. Capital market instruments are long term in nature

Debt instruments can be issued by privately owned companies, publicly owned companies and governments. Government of India issues infrastructure bonds and other bonds when there is a need for capital to be raised.

Equity instruments are those which grant the investor a specified share of ownership of assets of a company and right to proportionate part of any dividend declared. Shares issued by the company represent equity[4]. Shares can be either ordinary shares or preference shares.

---

[4] Dictionary meaning of equity is justness, value, worth, valuation.

Difference between Debt and Equity instruments

Sl. No	DEBT	EQUITY
1	Smallest unit of lending of the company.	Smallest unit of ownership of the company.
2	Holder of the instrument gets an assured interest for a stipulated period of time.	Holder of equity is being part of ownership of the company and hence he is part of the profit and loss of the company. Equity holder receives income when the company declares dividends. Losses or profits are limited to the extent of shares (ownership) held by the equity holder.
3	Debt instrument holder is a creditor from the company standpoint.	Equity holder is a part-owner of the company.
4	Lower in riskiness compared to Equity	Higher risk instrument

CHAPTER III

Concept Of Risk And Return

There always exists a chance (probability) of things not going as per our plan in every venture we undertake. This underlying uncertainty of things not going as per plan is called **risk**. It is something that each one of us thinks about and appreciates. Everyday examples are:

- *there is a risk that I might get late for my annual examination if my alarm clock doesn't work*
- *there is a risk of me being stumped if I attempt to hit a six by pushing forward*

Similarly, in every financial decision we do in our lives, there is a financial risk involved. For instance:

- *there is a risk of losing most of the invested money if the business that I started does not work*
- *there is a risk of losing my savings if I chose a highly-risky investment vehicle like Ponzi schemes (refer to Appendix II)*

Let's now look at RISK and RETURN matrix

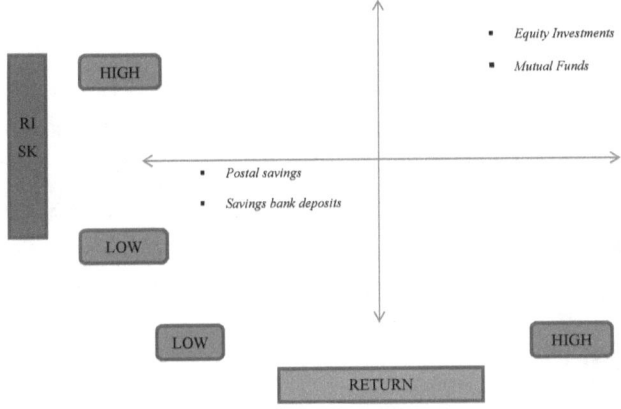

In the above diagram it can be seen that *"higher the risk, higher is the probability of higher return"*. In short, it is also referred to as **high risk-high return**. For instance, if you buy a lottery ticket for Rs.100 which has a jackpot prize of **Rs.1 crore** to one lucky winner, you can see that your Rs.100 investment can grow **100,000** times if you are going to be the lucky winner. But the chance that you may win the lucky jackpot prize is very slim. So, it is a highly risky investment[5] where you may stand to lose your entire investment but you may also turn out to be the jackpot winner for a huge return on your Rs.100 investment. Similarly, if you observe the **"High Risk-High Return"** quadrant in the matrix shown above you will see a typical set of financial instruments *viz*: Equity investments and

---

[5] We are not advocating lottery as an investment vehicle. It is not. The example is purely intended to explain the concept of high risk-high return in an easy to understand way.

Mutual fund investments which are considered to be risky but also have a greater chance of giving us above than normal returns.

Now, look at the bottom left corner of the matrix which is **"Low risk-Low return"** quadrant. The normal investment vehicles like fixed deposits, savings bank deposits, post-office deposits, National savings certificates and so on are examples of low risk-low return investment vehicles. Riskiness is measured on how safe the amount invested is.

Interest rates

If the amount invested is reasonably risk-free then it will normally have a low interest rate. Conversely, if the amount invested has a high risk of losing, then it will have high interest rates. It may be regarded as reward paid by an individual/organization for the use of money capital borrowed from another individual/ organization. *Interest is in some ways a reward to the risk taken (money invested).* For instance a post office savings deposit will earn about **6-8%** of interest which is pretty low compared to the high risk investment offers. The reason for this is postal deposits are funds that are controlled by the government and hence are considered to be secure investment. The basic assumption is that the government will always honor the investment made and will never default on the payments. So, the reward (interest rate) associated with it is low compared to others.

Risk free interest rates

As you move up the chain from low interest rates to higher, the money invested tends to be more unsafe. The interest rate earned on an investment with theoretically zero-risk involved is called ***"Risk-free interest rate"***. All the risk-free interest rate is stating is *"your money is super safe"* and hence the reward is low!!

Risk valuation by credit rating agencies and equity research organizations

Arriving at an assessment of the net value of the asset (debt or equity) where an investment is being planned by carefully examining the underlying risks of the assets is called *risk valuation*. The end state of this exercise leads to assigning a right risk rating to the asset. This is a good directional guidance to the end investors on the value of the underlying asset to decide on whether or not to invest.

Debt instruments are rated in the following manner by the Credit Rating Agencies[6](CRA's). The CRA's are neutral organizations and hence provide an assessment that is free of bias.

---

[6] CRISIL Ltd – www.crisil.com; Fitch Ratings India Pvt. Ltd. (www.fitchindia.com); ICRA Ltd. (www.icra.in); Credit Analysis and Research Ltd. (CARE) (www.careratings.com); Brickwork Ratings India Pvt. Ltd. (www.brickworksratings.com) are some of the key Credit Rating Agencies/Equity Research organizations for Debt and equity instruments in the Indian Capital Market.

Rating Symbol	Description (Probability of getting the return on investment as promised)	RISK
AAA[7]	Highest safety investment	Lowest
AA	High safety investment	Low
A	Adequate safety investment	Low
BBB	Moderate safety investment	Medium
BB	Inadequate safety investment	Medium
B	High Risk	High
C	Substantial Risk	Very High
D	Default	Highest Risk

Equity instruments are rated by the Equity Research organizations that provide bias-free grading of shares.

IPO Grading	Description (Probability of getting the return on investment as promised)	RISK
IPO Grade 1	Poor fundamentals	Highest
IPO Grade 2	Below average fundamentals	High
IPO Grade 3[8]	Average fundamentals	Medium
IPO Grade 4	Above average fundamentals	Low
IPO Grade 5	Strong fundamentals	Lowest

FINANCIAL RISK PROFILING

We just discussed that higher return on investment is normally coupled with higher risk. Not every individual or corporation likes to take risks. While some are happy with 8% returns on their capital, some look for 30% returns

---

[7] **AAA, AA, A, BBB** are ratings where the risks associated are permissible

[8] **IPO Grade 3, 4 and 5** are ratings with permissible risks

on their investments. Given that returns are directly proportional to risks implies that we discover the risk taking ability of an individual in order to suggest relevant investment avenues. Risk taking ability of an individual investor or a corporation is an objective evaluation of the "risk appetite" of the individual. This objective evaluation is called **FINANCIAL RISK PROFILING**. It involves answering a set of questionnaire broken into three broad categories:

1. **Risk required** – Risk associated with the return required to achieve the investor's goals from the financial resources available.
2. **Risk capacity** – Level of financial risk the investor can afford to take
3. **Risk tolerance** – Level of risk the investor is comfortable with.

This objective set of questionnaire is called "risk profiling questionnaire". Various flavors of the survey questionnaire exist but the end-result is to categorize the risk appetite of the investor into the following broad categories based on the answers provided to the objective questions. This evaluation is used to choose the right investment avenues as part of the financial planning process.

Financial Risk Category	Meaning	Recommended investment avenues based on Financial Risk Category
Risk averse	Investor who does not like to take financial risks and does not like uncertainties to his invested capital. He has the least risk tolerance.	1. Bonds 2. Fixed income securities 3. Government securities 4. Fixed deposits 5. Tax saving funds
Moderate Risk taker	Investor who is not Risk averse but does not like too many risks. His tolerance to risk is moderate.	1. A 60%-40% ratio in debt and equity investments. 2. Mutual Funds 3. Investments in Blue-Chip, large cap companies 4. Bonds 5. Fixed income securities 6. Government securities 7. Fixed deposits 8. Tax saving funds

Financial Risk Category	Meaning	Recommended investment avenues based on Financial Risk Category
Aggressive Risk taker	Investor who has high risk tolerance and does not mind losing part of his capital for a short period of time in view of a long term benefit.	1. Higher exposure to Small cap funds and Mid cap funds 2. Growth industries funds 3. Niche structured products aimed at volatile businesses 4. Commodities 5. 80% - 90% of the investments in equities and 10%-20% in debt instruments. 6. Investments in forex markets 7. Investments in derivative products (Futures and Options)

CHAPTER IV

Capital Markets – Process Of Getting A Company Listed In The Stock Exchange

Ram and his 4 partners, after a long thinking and planning process, decided to go with a plan to issue shares of their company *"**Retail Enterprises**"* through an IPO route in the Indian capital markets. They were guided by an **investment banker**[9]on the key actions that are to be taken to take a company public. The companies that issue their shares are called issuers and the process of issuing shares to public is known as public issue. This entire process involves various intermediaries like investment banker, bankers to the issue, underwriters, and registrars to the

---

[9] Investment banker or merchant banker helps companies through the legalities through the IPO process. It will help get various needed approvals as mandated by SEBI, provide valuation of the asset and come up with an offer price. They have the responsibility to make the IPO successful.

issue[10]. All these intermediaries are registered with SEBI and are required to abide by the prescribed norms to protect the investor.

Retail Enterprises chalks out the following plan to go public through an IPO (Initial Public Offer).

Sl. No.	Activity	Notes	Description
1	Appointment of Merchant/ Investment Bankers		To guide through the legalities of the IPO process. The Merchant bankers carry the risk of selling the securities to the public. They also engage to buy all the unsold shares in a process known as *underwriting*.
2	Pricing of securities being issued	Retail Enterprises was valued at **Rs.10**. **Rs.100 crore** is planned to be raised by issuing **10 crore** shares @ **Rs.10** per share.	With the help of merchant bankers the issue price of the security[11] is set.

---

[10] Registrar of the issue handles all the back-office transactions of the IPO on behalf of the issuer company.

[11] Shares issued are also called securities.

Sl. No.	Activity	Notes	Description
3	Communication/ Marketing of the issue	Of the **10 crore shares, 2.5 crore shares** are reserved for retail investors.	Media communications through newspapers, websites and television are issued by the issuer to ensure that all investors know enough about the offer. Essential elements that are communicated are the issue open and close dates.
4	Information on credit risk	Retail Enterprises got a credit rating for **IPO Grade 3** which puts it at medium risk	Key information manuals are released that document clearly the equity rating of the IPO as expressed by the rating agencies or equity research groups
5	Public issues opens in the Primary Market	The public issue is open for a minimum of 3 days.	All IPOs are issued through Primary Market where issuers directly contact the public at large to raise capital.
6	Collection of Money	This happens through the electronic clearance processes called ECS.	Currently, the IPO process is largely driven through a paperless online process and is a very easy process.

Sl. No.	Activity	Notes	Description
7	Minimum subscription	The minimum block of allotment is **100 shares** for retail investors[12].	The issue is said to be over-subscribed which means that subscriptions received for the IPO will be in excess of **10 crore** shares. If for instance, we receive subscriptions worth **40 crore** shares, then the issues is said to be over-subscribed **4 times**.

---

[12] Retail investors are small investors. A small investor can also be loosely defined as any investor buying and selling securities on a cash transaction.

Sl. No.	Activity	Notes	Description
8	Allotment of securities in Demat mode		The investors who have applied will get the allotment of shares. If the issue is over-subscribed, the allotments are done randomly through a computerized lucky draw process that randomly picks the lucky investors who will be allotted shares of the company (normally only for retail investors). The ones who do not get an allotment will have their investment refunded. For the institutional investors, the underwriters perform analysis on who can be given the shares of the company depending on the profiles of the institutional investors.

Sl. No.	Activity	Notes	Description
9	Listing of the security in Stock Exchanges (secondary market)	Retail Enterprises listed on the stock exchange with an initial price of **Rs.20,** twice the price at which it was offered.	Secondary market is where the stocks get listed in the stock exchange. From the day it is listed on the secondary market, the shares of the company can be freely traded (bought and sold) among the shareholders. For instance, if an investor Guru was allotted 100 shares of Retail Enterprises at Rs.10, he can sell those 100 shares at the market price of Rs.20 on the day it is listed on the exchange thus realizing a profit of Rs.1000 immediately.

Retail Enterprises, once listed on the stock exchange is said to be a publicly listed company. Investors can trade in the share of *Retail Enterprises* as and when they wish.

IPO Pricing

Broadly there are two methods to decide on IPO pricing. They are:

1. Fixed price method
2. Book building method

Fixed price method

This is a straightforward method of deciding on issue price. This is generally arrived at by discussions with company by the merchant banks. Frequently, the issue price is underpriced to generate investor interest. In the example detailed, *Retail Enterprises* went ahead with a fixed price method of IPO pricing.

Book building method

This is a method where investor data is analyzed by the merchant banks after providing guidance on a broad price range of the offer. Imagine if *Retail Enterprises* came up with an IPO stating that the price range of the offer will be between Rs.12 and Rs.20. Once the IPO window opens, investors start bidding the offer at various price levels. The underwriters and the issuer then look at this demand data to decide on the issue price of the stock which is then announced. This is called book-building method.

CHAPTER V

Indian Capital Market Structure And Functions

Capital markets are an institutional arrangement to borrow and lend money for a longer period of time. **Money markets** on the other hand are designed to borrow or lend money for a short period of time. Financial dealings are always sensitive transactions and hence there needs to exist a strong governance and regulatory mechanism to ensure that the transactions are legitimate and no unethical practices are observed. Protection of investor interest is of utmost importance to ensure that there is a continuous flow of investments to the capital market. This function is undertaken by the capital market regulator SEBI.

The Capital Market Regulator – SEBI

SEBI (Securities and Exchange Board of India) is the regulator for the securities market in India. It was established in the year 1988 and given statutory powers on 12 April 1992 through the SEBI Act of 1992. SEBI was set up to protect investor interests, regulate and develop capital market in

India by SEBI Act 1992, passed by the Indian parliament. It started operations in 1994. Headquartered in Mumbai with regional offices in Delhi, Chennai and Ahmedabad, SEBI educates investor and regulates Indian capital market.

The **SEBI** is managed by a **Chairman** plus an **8** member board constituted of the following members:

1. The **chairman** who is nominated by Union Government of India.
2. **Two members**, i.e., Officers from Union Finance Ministry.
3. **One member** from the Reserve Bank of India.
4. **Five members** nominated by Union government of India of whom three work as whole-time directors

Key SEBI Functions

Capital market constitutes of three groups of people whose interest has to be catered to by SEBI

- The Issuers of securities (e.g. companies like Retail Enterprises that was discussed earlier)
- The investors (e.g. large investors, small investors, foreign institutional investors)
- The market intermediaries (e.g. banks, mutual funds, merchant banks, Venture Capitalists)

Capital Market – Functional classification

Functionally, capital market can be categorized into four entities as follows:

1. **Gilt Market** – This is the market for government and semi-government securities (like GoI bonds, infrastructure bonds, RBI bonds and so on) which carry fixed interest rates.

2. **Industrial Securities Market (Stock Market)** – This market deals with equities and debentures in which shares and debentures of existing companies are traded and shares/debentures of new companies are traded. This is also called **Stock Market.**

3. **Development Financial Institutions** – The financial institutions of the likes of IFCI, ICICI, IDBI, SIDBI, IRBI, UTI, LIC and so on were set up to meet the medium and long-term requirements of industry, trade and agriculture. These financial institutions are called public sector financial institutions.

4. **Financial Intermediaries** – The financial intermediaries include merchant or investment banks, Mutual Fund houses, leasing companies who help in mobilizing savings and supplying funds to capital market.

Key functions of capital markets

We have now seen how capital markets facilitate capital exchange between the investors and the capital seeking companies. Following are the key functions of capital markets:

1. **Mobilization of savings and acceleration of capital formation** – Capital market as an institution helps bring the investors to the right place where money is needed to be invested. This accelerates the capital formation process.

2. **Raising long-term capital** – Stock exchanges ensure that there is continuous flow of funds by allowing trading of securities giving rise to a sustained long-term capital generation.

3. **Promotion of industrial growth** – Stock exchange is a central capital market where capital is transferred to the industrial sector of the economy. Existence of this channel encourages investors to invest in productive channels. This activity stimulates industrial growth providing the necessary capital for expansion.

4. **Ready and continuous market** – Stock exchange makes investment in securities more liquid as compared to other assets.

5. **Reliable guide to performance** – The capital market is a barometer to industrial performance. It serves as a reliable guide to the performance and financial position of corporates, and thereby promotes efficiency.

6. **Proper channelization of funds** – The prevailing market price of a security and relative yield are the guiding factors for the people to channelize their funds in a particular company. This ensures effective utilization of funds in the public interest.

7. **Foreign Capital** – Capital markets enable foreign capital generation through Foreign Institutional

Investors (FIIs) and Foreign Direct Investment (FDI) in certain sectors. Indian firms are able to generate capital funds from overseas markets by way of bonds and other securities.

8. **Easy Liquidity** – With the help of secondary market, investors can sell off their holdings and convert them into liquid cash. Commercial banks also allow investors to withdraw their deposits, as and when they are in need of funds.

Safeguarding investor interest

For any country to witness growth, we need investor confidence in the system. This, to a certain extent, is measurable by how strict the rules and regulations are and how efficiently they are put to practice in ensuring it is a fair trade. An investor will part with his money only when he knows it is safe enough to invest. Legislations have been introduced from the last few decades to address this issue of safeguarding investor interest. The most important of them are:

1. **The Companies Act, 1956** – this act sets aside guidelines for code of conduct for the corporate sector with respect to disclosures, transfer, issuance and allotment of securities.

2. **The Securities Contracts (Regulation) Act, 1956** – sets aside guidelines for security transactions.

3. **The SEBI Act, 1992** – Act introduced the governing body for securities market

4. **The Depositories Act, 1996** – sets rules for dematerialized securities and enabled rapid digitization of markets.

5. **The Prevention of Money Laundering Act (PMLA), 2002**

CHAPTER VI

Stock Exchange Or Industrial Securities Market

Stock exchange facilitates the trading (buying and selling) of shares, bonds and debentures. Stock exchanges also provide facilities for issue and redemption of securities and other financial instruments, and capital events including the payment of income and dividends.

Primary Market and Secondary Market

Stock markets can be classified into Primary and Secondary markets. Primary market is the market for new shares. Just like we saw in the example case of *Retail Enterprises*, the first time issuer of shares in the market works his way through the Primary Market. On the other hand, Secondary Market is the market of existing traded securities of companies. Post listing, the stock (securities) is traded in the secondary market.

Stock Exchanges in India

India has two major stock exchanges. They are:

1. **BSE** – Bombay Stock Exchange – Established on July 9th, 1875 in Mumbai. It is one of the oldest Asian Stock Exchanges. [Website: www. bseindia.com]
2. **NSE** – National Stock Exchange – Established in 1992, Mumbai. [Website: www.nseindia.com]

While BSE is the oldest stock exchange in India, NSE is the largest stock exchange in terms of daily turnover and number of trades.

Trading mechanism in Stock Exchanges

With the advent of advanced computing solutions, trading at stock exchanges is completely driven by automated trading computers who do the order matching before executing orders. The orders should be placed through a SEBI and stock exchange registered stock broker.

Settlement Cycle and Trading Hours

Equity transactions currently follow a T + 2 settlement cycle. This means that if one has sold shares worth Rs.5000 on Monday then the money will be credited to his or her account on Wednesday of that week. The trading hours on stock exchanges takes place between **9:15 AM and 3:30 PM (IST)**, Mondays through Friday of the week.

Dematerialization

In earlier days, a physical share certificate of the company whose share has been purchased would be issued to the purchaser. This was called materialized form. Nowadays, though, with advancements in digital machinery, no physical share certificates are issued. Instead, shares are deposited in digital format in the account called dematerialized account (or DEMAT account) of the purchaser. This is called dematerialization and the account is called DEMAT Account. DEMAT account is a must-have to trade in stocks. This digitization effort has brought lots of efficiencies to the trading process and has reduced time and effort for each trade. Even physical certificates of Govt. Securities debt instruments and all such instruments can be held in a single demat A/c. (In other words holding shares and other investment in electronic mode). The dematerialization can be reversed if one wishes so by re-materialization. The depository's act of 1996 has given the investor an option to hold securities in physical or Demat-form but nowadays almost all securities are held in dematerialized form.

Depository Participant (DP)

A **Depository Participant (DP)** is described as an agent of the depository. They are the intermediaries between the depository and the investors. The relationship between the DPs and the depository is governed by an agreement made between the two under the Depositories Act. In a strictly legal sense, a DP is an entity who is registered as such with **SEBI under the sub section 1A of Section 12**

of the SEBI Act. As per the provisions of this Act, a **DP** can offer depository-related services only after obtaining a certificate of registration from SEBI.

There are two depositories in India. One is the **National Securities Depository Limited (NSDL)**[13] and the other is **the Central Depository Service (India) Limited (CDSL)**[14]. Every Depository Participant (DP) needs to be registered under this depository before it begins its operation or trade in the market.

Functions of the depository include:

1. **Dematerialization** – converting physical certificates to electronic form
2. **Rematerialization** – converting electronic to physical certificates
3. **Transfer of securities** – change of beneficial ownership
4. **Settlement of trades** – settlement of trades done on exchange connected to depository

Stock Broker

A stockbroker is a regulated professional individual, usually associated with a brokerage firm or broker-dealer, who buys and sells stocks and other securities for both retail and institutional clients, through a stock exchange or over the counter, in return for a fee or commission. He is registered with one of the SEBI

---

[13] https://nsdl.co.in
[14] https://www.cdslindia.com

depositories by complying with the essential obligations of being a registered member.

Sub-Broker

A *sub-broker* is any person who is not a trading member of a Stock Exchange but who acts on behalf of a trading member as an agent or otherwise for assisting investors in dealing in securities through such trading members. All sub-brokers are required to obtain a Certificate of Registration from SEBI without which they are not permitted to deal in securities. SEBI has directed that no Trading member shall deal with a person who is acting as a sub-broker unless he is registered with SEBI and it shall be the responsibility of the trading member to ensure that his clients are not acting in the capacity of a sub-broker unless they are registered with SEBI as a sub-broker. It is mandatory for trading members to enter into an agreement that lays down the rights and responsibilities of trading members as well as sub-brokers.

Market Capitalization[15]

It is the total currency value of all the company's outstanding shares. Market capitalization is calculated by multiplying a company's shares outstanding by the current market price of one share. This is a proxy to company's size. Higher the market capitalization, higher is the size of the company. In the example we discussed the market cap of *Retail Enterprises* will be 10 crores (outstanding

---

[15] Also called market cap

shares) * Rs.20 (closing price of day 1) which is Rs.200 crores.

Based on the Market capitalization of companies, there are 3 segments of stocks that have been defined. They are:

Market Cap category	Definition
Large-cap[16] stocks	Stocks whose market capitalization ranges from **Rs.200 billion to Rs.3500 billion.**
Medium-cap stocks	Stocks whose market capitalization ranges from **Rs.50 billion to Rs.200 billion.**
Small-cap stocks	Stocks whose market capitalization ranges from **less than Rs.50 billion**

Large-cap stocks are shares of usually large and well established companies that have a strong market presence and are generally considered safe investments. Most of the large cap companies have good disclosures and therefore there is no dearth of information for an investor looking into them. Large companies such as Reliance, Infosys, TCS and Wipro are classified as large cap stocks. These companies have been around in the industry long enough and have firmly established themselves as leading players. Their stocks are publicly traded and have large market capitalizations.

Mid-cap stocks are shares of mid-size companies that are relatively more risky than large cap as investment options, yet are not as risky as small cap stocks. When one invests in mid-caps for the long term, he may be investing

---

[16] Cap here means Market Capitalization

in companies that could become tomorrow's runaway success stories. Generally speaking, mid cap stocks as an investment can bring you higher returns in 3 to 5 years as opposed to their big brother large cap stocks that can bring you moderate returns during this timeframe.

Small-cap stocks are shares of smaller companies with smaller revenue and client bases. Small cap stocks are potentially big gainers as they are yet to be discovered within the sector and can show growth potential in large numbers once they are discovered in the market.

Stock Index[17] (Stock Indices)

Stock index is a number used to show the current value of shares on the stock market based on the prices and the selected number of shares (either NSE or BSE). An index is a basket of identified stocks and its value is computed taking using a weighed price technique. The BSE index is called **SENSEX** and the NSE main index is called **NIFTY**.

1. **SENSEX[18]** stock index is based on a basket of **30 stocks** across different industry verticals.

---

[17] Think of INDEX as a number which tells you something that can lead to action. Just like a thermometer gives you an indication of body temperature which will help figure out if one is running a temperature or not, an INDEX provides you an indication of whether or not the industries are performing well in a country.

[18] SENSEX word is derived from **SENS**itive ind**EX**. It was introduced on Jan 1, 1986. Base value of the index is set to 100 and the base year is 1978-79.

2. **NIFTY**[19]stock index is based on a basket of **50 stocks** across different industry verticals.

On any trading day, the indexes SENSEX and NIFTY are computed in every 5-15 second interval.

BSE has about **5000 listed companies** while **NSE** has about **1700 companies** listed. There are a lot of common stocks traded both in NSE and BSE.

Stock market index are useful for a number of reasons as listed below:

1. They provide a historical comparison of returns on money invested in the stock market against other forms of investments such as GOLD or Debt.
2. Stock index can be used as standard against which to compare the performance of an equity fund.
3. It is a lead indicator of the performance of the overall economy or a sector of the economy.
4. Modern financial applications such as Index Funds, Index Futures, Index Options play an important role in financial investments and risk management.

---

[19] NIFTY was coined by combining words NATIONAL and FIFTY. Base of the index is set as 1000 and the base year is set to 1995. Nifty is calculated using 50 top stocks across 24 different sectors and those stocks that are actively traded.

Broad Market Indices

While **SENSEX** (in BSE) and **NIFTY** (in NSE) are the two most important indices that are performance barometers of the entire range of stocks, there exists, other indices that have been constructed to measure specific group of market segments or stocks. Some of the indexes created for this purpose in NSE[20] are:

Broad market index	Purpose
CNX NIFTY JUNIOR	It has the 50 top liquid[21] stocks from various sectors that are not part of the main NIFTY index
CNX 100[22]	It is a diversified 100 stock index accounting for 38 sectors of the economy. For every 100 rupees traded in NSE, about **68 rupees** are from the stocks that are part of CNX 100 index
CNX 200	This index reflects the behavior and performance of top 200 companies measured by market capitalization. The companies are all positive net-worth companies. For every 100 rupees traded in NSE, about **85 rupees** are from the stocks that are part of CNX 200 index
CNX 500	This is a very broad based benchmark index of the Indian Capital Market. It represents 96% of the market capitalization of the stocks listed as on June 30, 2014. For every 100 rupees traded in NSE, about **96 rupees** are from the stocks that are part of CNX 500 index.

[20] BSE will also have similar or slightly differently defined broad market indices. The underlying idea remains the same.
[21] Liquid stocks means most traded stocks. These are stocks that have large number of transactions on a daily basis.
[22] This index is owned and managed by India Index Services and Products Ltd. (IISL)

Broad market index	Purpose
NIFTY MIDCAP 50	Mid-Cap segment is always considered an attractive segment as it witnesses strong growth. This index was constructed to provide a barometer to measure the growth in the mid-cap segment of the market. Launched in 2010, this tracks about top 7.5% of the market capitalization. For every 100 rupees traded in NSE, about **17 rupees** are from the stocks that are part of NIFTY MIDCAP 50 index.
CNX MIDCAP	Similar to the NIFTY MIDCAP 50 index, this index tracks Mid-cap stocks. It is formed by about 14% of the market capitalization stocks. For every 100 rupees traded in NSE, about **22 rupees** are from the stocks that are part of CNX MIDCAP index.
CNX SMALLCAP Index	This index reflects the behavior and performance of the small-cap segment of the financial market. This comprises of 100 tradable, listed companies. It represents about 3.5% of the market capitalization. For every 100 rupees traded in NSE, about **9 rupees** are from the stocks that are part of CNX Smallcap index.

Industry Sectors and Sector Indices

Stock markets comprises of stocks that are from various sectors of the economy like financial sector, engineering sector, automobile sector, FMCG sector, Energy sector and so on. These are called industry sectors and are also referred to as verticals. Normally, there are multiple companies within an industry sector. The sector indices constructed provide a good basis of understanding how an industry sector is performing. This in turn helps in understanding which specific companies are doing well and the ones that are not. It also helps discover sector specific issues.

NSE has the following sectoral indices constructed.

Sectoral index	Number of companies included in the index	Few companies that are part of the index computation	Purpose
CNX AUTO Index	15	• Tata Motors • Ashok Leyland • Bajaj Auto • Apollo Tyres • Maruti Suzuki	Designed to reflect the behavior and performance of Automobiles sector.
CNX BANK Index	12	• Axis Bank • SBI • Canara Bank • ICICI Bank • HDFC Bank	It comprises of the most liquid and large capitalized Indian banking stocks.
CNX ENERGY Index	10	• NTPC • Tata Power • Indian Oil Corporation • GAIL • Reliance Industries	Energy sector is one of the most important sectors that are crucial to development in India. Companies belonging to Petroleum, Gas and Power sectors for part of the ENERGY index.

Sectoral index	Number of companies included in the index	Few companies that are part of the index computation	Purpose
CNX FINANCE Index	15	• SBI • LIC Housing • Axis Bank • IDFC • Shriram Transport Finance	This index measures performance of Indian Financial market. It comprises of banks, financial institutions and housing finance.
CNX FMCG Index	15	• Colgate • ITC • Emami • Marico • Hindustan Unilever	Track progress and performance of FMCG segment. FMCG is Fast Moving Consumer Goods – Industries that manufacture FMCG items like Brush, Pastes, Biscuits, Oil, Soap, Shampoo and so on which are products of mass consumption, non-durable and consumed rapidly.

Sectoral index	Number of companies included in the index	Few companies that are part of the index computation	Purpose
CNX IT Index	20	• Infosys • Justdial • TCS • Wipro • NIIT	Tracks performance of Indian Information Technology industry.
CNX MEDIA Index	11	• Network18 Media • Sun Network • TV18 • PVR • Zee Entertainment	Tracks media and entertainment sector of Indian industry.
CNX METAL Index	15	• Tata Steel • Coal India • Steel Authority of India • Hindalco • National Alluminium	Tracks metal sector of Indian industry.
CNX PHARMA Index	10	• CIPLA • Divi's Labs • Glaxosmithkline • Piramal Enterprises • Dr. Reddy's Labs	Healthcare as a sector is one of the most important for the overall progress of the country.

Sectoral index	Number of companies included in the index	Few companies that are part of the index computation	Purpose
CNX PSU BANK Index	12	• SBI • Allahabad Bank • Bank of Baroda • Syndicate Bank • Oriental Bank of Commerce	Tracks Public Sector Banks (Nationalized banks). This will help banks get to build a competitive edge against the private banks in servicing customers.
CNX REALTY Index	10	• Sobha Ltd. • Unitech Ltd. • Indiabulls Ltd. • Delta Corp Ltd. • Godrej Properties Ltd.	Tracks performance of Real Estate sector. As real estate is witnessing tremendous growth this is an useful index to track progress of realty sector.

Market Participants

The various kinds of investors that participate (trade) in the stock exchanges are:

1. **Retail investors** – Individual investors who buy and sell securities for their personal account, and not for another company or organization.

2. **Institutional Investors** – An institutional investor is an investor, such as a bank, a private firm, insurance company, retirement fund, hedge fund, or mutual fund that is financially sophisticated and makes large investments, often held in very large portfolios of investments. Because of their sophistication, institutional investors may often participate in private placements of securities, in which certain aspects of the securities laws may be inapplicable.

3. **Foreign Institutional Investors (FIIs)** – An investor or investment fund that is from or registered in a country outside of the one in which it is currently investing. Institutional investors include hedge funds, insurance companies, pension funds and mutual funds. Recently, FIIs and FDIs have been clubbed together through an amendment.

Trader and investor

There are a variety of people transacting in the capital markets. The most commonly heard categories are traders and investors. Each one of them is trying to profit from the market but have fundamentally different approaches to achieve the profit goal. We will try to understand the key differences between these two categories.

Criteria	Trader	Investor
Investment time horizon	Short term (less than 1 year)	Long term (More than 1 year)
Transactions	Numerous. Given that the trader is involved in frequent buying and selling.	Less frequent churn
Ideology	Speculative. They take small and frequent profits by frequent trades.	Company fundamentals and strategic decisions. Investors seek higher returns in the long run.
Investment method	Based on technical analysis and news	Based on fundamental analysis of companies

There are further categories of traders that can be made depending on the investment time horizon parameter. They are:

1. **Position Trader:** Category of traders who hold positions for few months.
2. **Swing Trader:** Traders who hold positions ranging from a few days to a few weeks.
3. **Day Trader:** Traders who hold positions for a day and square off their positions.
4. **Scalp Trader:** Traders who hold positions for a few seconds to minutes.

Delisting

Delisting refers to the process of removal of a listed security from the exchange on which it trades. Until now, we have seen how a company can make itself a public company by seeking public investments through IPO. The company thereby will be listed in the stock exchange where it can be freely traded. Every publicly traded company or a listed company has to abide by the rules of the market regulator SEBI which includes publication of quarterly results before the deadline, adherence to disclosures and so on.

Delisting can happen because of the reasons mentioned below:

1. **Compulsory delisting:** The listed company failed to fulfill to the SEBI's regulatory norms of a listed company and has been penalized by delisting the stock.
2. **Voluntary delisting:** Company is going private as it has bought back all the shares from the shareholders and can no longer be traded.

Divestment

Process of selling an asset (or a portion of the overall asset) is called **divestment**[23]. It is the opposite of investment. Suppose *Retail Enterprises* had various number of retail businesses say, footwear, brokerage, jewellery, cosmetics, and agriculture equipment and so on. Suppose it takes a conscious decision of getting away from the agriculture equipment business for reasons that it has not been profitable and they are not growing in that segment. *Retail Enterprises* then will attempt to look at selling that business to a market player willing to buy that business.

---

[23] Government of India recently decided to divest 5% of its stake in SAIL (Steel Authority of India Ltd.).

CHAPTER VII

Getting Started With Stock Trading

Until now, we have seen a typical business which wants to raise capital and how it manages to do so using the mechanism of Indian Capital Markets. The next logical question we will tackle now is to provide an investor viewpoint of this process. How does typical investor who is interested in owning a share of *Retail Enterprises* manage to do so?

In this chapter, we will see how one can get started with stock trading. We will discuss step by step process and the pre-requisites of getting oneself ready to trade in the market.

Step 1 – PAN Card (Permanent Account Number)

One will need to have the PAN card to start trading in capital markets. The PAN card is issued by the Income Tax office and can be done by submitting an online application (form 49A) at the following NSDL website. [PAN Card Link: https://tin.tin.nsdl.com/pan/form49A.html]

Step 2 – Bank Account

Share transactions, as discussed earlier, are completely digitized and hence most of it happens through Electronic Clearance Systems. It is imperative that a person wanting to start stock trading as an investor needs to have a Bank Account with one of the nationalized or private sector banks. Generally, accounts with Grameen Banks, co-operative society banks do not work well for stock trading and hence it is advisable to open accounts with nationalized banks (like SBI, SBM, SYNDICATE, CANARA, CORPORATION and so on) or private banks (like ICICI, HDFC, CITI, YES, FEDERAL and so on).

Step 3 – Additional facilities required in your bank account

While getting a bank account opened, you should ensure that the following services are provided by the bank

1. Online banking
2. Mobile banking
3. Debit card

Step 4 – Demat account and trading account

A Demat and trading account will enable stock trading. Normally these two accounts are opened together with a single broker. There is wide range of choice available to get the Demat and trading accounts opened. A few known ones are Sharekhan, ICICIDirect, Tradejini and so on. Apart from these, there are a number of other local broker offices in most of the towns where you can open the Demat and trading account. Most of the banks also provide Demat and trading account services now. Brokerage charged by each of the brokers vary. It takes only a couple of days to open a Demat and trading account with any broker or sub-broker. You can open multiple Demat accounts with different service providers if needed but this is not a recommended practice as maintenance cost increases.

Some documents that need to be provided while opening a Demat account are:

1. Signed agreement (in prescribed form) which details your and DP's rights and duties. One can have an account opened either single or jointly.
2. Proof of identity
3. PAN Card (must)
4. Address proof (Ration Card, Voters ID, Bank Pass Book) or any other identity proof
5. KYC (Know your Client) form
6. Email Id.

Share trading these days are done using online trading platforms offered by NSE. NSE introduced a nationwide on line fully automated Screen Based Trading (SBTs) system where a member can punch with the computer, quantities of securities and price at which he/she likes to transact and the transactions are executed as soon as it finds a matching sale or buy orders from the counter party. SBT electronically matches orders on a strict price/ time priority and hence cuts down time, cost and risk of error as well as fraud resulting in improved operational efficiency (here the identity of either the buyer or seller is not revealed). NSE's server network is connected through **Very Small Aperture Terminal (VSATs)** installed at all broker offices. These VSAT terminals are used to punch deals (BUY and SELL). **NEAT (National Exchange for Automated Trading)** system is trading software.

It is vital that one goes through the trading software provided by the service provider before you open an account. This will require **basic computer knowledge** to understand trading software to perform trading actions using it.

Step 5 – Basic understanding of stocks

In 2005, the SEBI established the National Institute of Securities Markets (**NISM**[24]) in Mumbai. Both SEBI and NISM promote security market education and research. It is worthwhile to spend time to understand stocks and how they work by reading websites, books or attending training sessions.

---

[24] http://www.nseindia.com/education/content/module_nism.htm

CHAPTER VIII

Basic Trading Concepts Explained

In this chapter we will go through some illustrative transactions that will help bring out some of the important stock market concepts associated with stock trading.

Stock Market Equilibrium

Scenario – In a stock market on any given day,

$$\textbf{Total number of stocks sold = Total}$$
$$\textbf{number of stocks bought}[25]$$

Explanation –

1. This means that for every stock we buy, there is a seller in the market who wants to sell it at a price

---

[25] There is one exception to this rule but largely this equation is true. The exception arises from the open position transactions but they are few in number. The total shares traded remain same but at various price points.

point. If the buyer agrees to the seller's price point and quantity, he buys the share. Else the seller cannot sell the share and it remains with him. It is important to understand that each transaction has a **BUY** part and a **SELL** part to it.

2. Once a company, for instance, as seen in the example *Retail Enterprises* raises the capital of Rs.100 crore, the company shares are traded in the stock market. All that happens is that the shares of the company are changing hands from one set of shareholders to another or the existing set of shares are getting distributed among multiple shareholders at different prices as controlled by the demand and supply economics of the investors which in turn depends on market sentiment. The Buyer becomes the new shareholder of the company and the Seller parts with his complete ownership of the company or part ownership of the company depending on whether he has sold all of his shares or a part of his holdings respectively.

3. It is important to note that these monetary transactions occurring because of BUY and SELL in the stock market of *Retail Enterprises* or any other company do not enter into the books of the company. For instance, *Retail Enterprises* raised **Rs.100 crore** from the IPO and that's the only money it gets and is part of the shareholders' equity in its balance sheet. All the other BUY and SELL transactions that happen in the stock market are between two kinds of investors.

a. **Buyers:** The investors or current shareholders who want to be shareholders or increase their investment in the company are wanting to BUY shares of the company

b. **Sellers:** The current shareholders of the company who want to SELL either part of their investment in the company or want to SELL all of their investment in the company.

4. Total number of shares issued by the company remains constant and cannot change unless the company introduces additional shares in the market. In our earlier example, we have seen that Retail Enterprises had an IPO with **10 crore shares** of Rs.10 each. The **10 crore shares** are what are traded in the market between the different shareholders viz: Small investors and Institutional investors. The trades happen at various price points depending on prevailing market sentiment, company performance, future potential, news, macroeconomic situation and so on but the total number of shares remains the same.

Rights Issue

Scenario –

1. *Retail Enterprises* board of directors decided that they need additional capital funding for another expansion plan.
2. Money capital required is pegged at Rs.75 crore.

3. They propose to go with a RIGHTS issue of an additional **3 crore shares** that they will offer to existing shareholders of the company as of date, called Record Date of 1-Dec-2014 at a discounted price of Rs.25 per share.
4. The market price of the stock on the day of this announcement was Rs.28.
5. RIGHTS issue can be subscribed to by existing shareholders in blocks of **100 shares**.

Explanation – RIGHTS issue is an invitation to the existing shareholders of the company to purchase additional new shares of the company. It is called RIGHTS because it is offered to existing shareholders and they are free to exercise their right. They can do the following:

a. Apply for additional shares and pay the additional amount of money.
b. Do nothing.
c. Renounce the rights in favor of another person who is interested in the offer and can apply for the rights issue.

1. RIGHTS issues are normally at a discounted price to the market price. This is done to provide an additional incentive to the existing shareholders to invest additional amount in the company.
2. The same procedures followed in the case of IPO are followed. The merchant banker helps the company by owning the responsibilities of raising the capital.

3. The record date set by the company is the cut-off date to ascertain the eligible list of current shareholders of the company to the RIGHTS issue.

4. A few reasons why a company chooses to go for a RIGHTS issue are:

   a. Raise additional capital.

   b. It has a large debt which it needs to address quickly as the company cannot borrow additional money from creditors.

5. It is important to understand why the company is coming up with a RIGHTS issue as the share value is set to dilute due to additional inflow of shares in the market post the RIGHTS issue.

FPO – Follow on Public Offer

Scenario –

1. *Retail Enterprises* board of directors decided that they need additional capital funding to further diversify their business and pay off some of the debt.

2. Capital required is pegged at Rs.50 crore.

3. They propose to go with a FPO issue selling an additional 7% stake in the company.

4. The price band of the FPO is Rs.28 to Rs.32.

5. Retail investors will be given a 10% discount on the final offer price determined by book-building process.

6. Employees of the company have 0.5% of the issue reserved.

Explanation – FPO[26] is issued by companies those are already traded in the secondary markets. It is open for all investors to invest. The follow on public offer is issued by companies who need additional funding for a variety of reasons. Some of the reasons can be:

    a.   Business expansion
    b.   Strategic investments
    c.   Debt pay-off

Open Offer

Scenario –

1. *Retail Enterprises,* which has a 15% stake in another listed company called *A-to-Z Ventures,* wants to increase its stake to 35% in *A-to-Z Ventures.*
2. They go with an open offer at a price of Rs.32 per share which is a 12.5% premium to the last six months average price of Rs.28 per share after consultations with the merchant banker.
3. Promoters of *Retail Enterprises* approach the merchant banker. Newspaper announcements are made with the letter of intent addressed to the existing shareholders of *A-to-Z ventures.* SEBI website lists the details on the open offer including a letter of offer and form of acceptance.

---

[26] Recently in December 2013, Power Grid Corporation of India came up with an FPO selling 17% stake in the company to public. The price band of the issue was in the price range of Rs.85-Rs.90 per share.

4. Disclosures include a business justification, details of the offer, price point details, number of shares to be acquired, acquisition purpose and future plans.

Explanation –

1. This is called an open offer. When a company/individual investor/any legal entity wants to increase their stake in another listed company (normally beyond 15%), they go for an open offer.
2. The open offer is generally at a premium price to the last 6 months average trading price of the underlying stock (in this case, *A-to-Z Ventures*) of the company to encourage current shareholders to relinquish their ownership.
3. This is slightly different from RIGHTS issue because in rights issue, company is raising capital by selling additional shares typically at a discounted price to the market price to encourage people to invest.
4. This is also called Takeovers & substantial acquisition of shares. This can be done by a company/individual/any legal entity.

Face Value (or Par Value), At Par and Premium

Scenario – Retail Enterprises IPO discussed earlier had 10 crore shares offered at Rs.10 each. The face value of the stock was Rs.10 and the offer was said to be at par.

Explanation –

1. Face value of a share is the default value of one unit share of the company. In this case, 10 crore shares were offered and each share's face value was Rs.10. **Face value of the share is Rs.10.**
2. It is also called as **PAR Value.**
3. If an IPO is offered at a price equivalent to the face value of the share, then the offer is said to be **AT PAR.**
4. Suppose, *Retail Enterprises* had offered **10 crore shares of face value Rs.10** at Rs.15 instead of Rs.10, then the difference is said to be share **PREMIUM**. In this case, the shares are said to be at Rs.5 premium to the face value.

Dividend

Scenario –

1. On 29-JUL-2014, Board of directors of *Retail Enterprises* approved **dividend** payment of **20%** on the face value of the share.
2. The record date is set to be 29-AUG-2014.
3. Ex-dividend date is set to be 27-AUG-2014.

Explanation –

1. A **dividend** is a payment made by a company to its shareholders, usually as a distribution of profits. When a company earns a surplus, it can either reinvest it back into growing the business or pass

on the goodness to its shareholders. The portion of money reinvested in the business is called **retained earnings** and the one that is distributed among the shareholders is called **dividend**.

2. **Dividend** is declared as a percentage of the face value of the share. In this case, 20% dividend implies that the dividend amount is Rs.2 per share[27]. If I have 100 shares of *Retail Enterprises*, I will get a dividend of **Rs.200** provided I have the shares with me on the record date as specified by the notification. In this case, the record date is **29-AUG-2014**.

3. In this example scenario, 29-Jul-2014 is called the Declaration Date

4. Ex-Dividend date is normally 2 working days before the record date. Anyone purchasing shares on or after Ex-dividend date will not be eligible for the dividend amount.

Bonus Shares

Scenario –

1. On 14-JAN-2014, Board of directors of *Retail Enterprises* approved **BONUS** issue of shares in the ratio 1:5.

2. The record date is set to be 11-FEB-2014.

---

[27] 20% of Rs.10 is Rs.2. Rs.10 is the face value per share of the company *Retail Enterprises*

Explanation –

1. Bonus shares are free shares issued by the company to its existing shareholders. Unlike RIGHTS issue, bonus shares are distributed free of cost.

2. Bonus shares are issued in a ratio of the shares an investor holds. The ratio here is 1:5 which means that for every 5 shares held by the investor, 1 free share will be given. For instance, if I have 100 shares as on the record date then I will get 20 additional free shares as part of the bonus Issue.

3. All the investors holding the shares as on the record date set by the company are eligible for the issuance of bonus shares.

4. Companies pay bonus shares sometimes in place of dividends for tax purposes. Dividend payouts require the company to pay a dividend distribution tax. Bonus shares are excluded from tax payouts.

5. Bonus shares increase the shares in circulation in stock market. For instance, the bonus issue of **1:5** by *Retail Enterprises* will increase the number of shares by **20%** in the market.

6. Due to an increase in shares in the market, the share price comes down almost in the same proportion in the market.

7. **Earnings per Share (EPS)** of the company which is defined as {Income / [Total Outstanding Shares]} decreases post bonus because the denominator has increased.

Stock Split

Scenario –

1. On 05-JUN-2014, Board of directors of a large company approved for a STOCK SPLIT to have the face value to be Rs.10 from the current Rs.100. This is called 10 for 1 split.
2. The record date is set to be 04-JUL-2014.
3. Share prices of the company have been trading at about **Rs.9,000 per share** for some time now.

Explanation –

1. A Stock split is a decision by the company board of directors to increase the number of shares that are outstanding by issuing more shares to current shareholders. In this example, every shareholder will get 9 additional stocks to one stock that he current has. Suppose an investor has 100 stocks of this company as of the record date, he will get 900 additional shares making his total share-holding in the company to 1000.
2. The total outstanding shares will increase 10 fold after the stock split. Here the face value of the stock which was Rs.100 before will now become Rs.10.
3. The share prices will decrease in exactly the same proportion as well such that the Market Capitalization ({Number of Outstanding Shares * Price}] remains constant before and after the stock split.

4. Stock split is usually done by companies that have seen their share price increase to levels that are either too high or are beyond the price levels of similar companies in their sector. In this case, high prices pose difficulty to investors to buy shares of this company. Once the stock is split, the prices will be reduced (10 fold in this case) and will begin in the range of Rs.900 per share which makes it relatively easier and affordable to trade.

5. A stock split can also result in a stock price increase following the decrease immediately after the split. Price affordability brings new cheer in stock traders and investors. This increases demand which consequently increases prices. Stock split also indicates to the market that the share prices have been increasing steadily and will continue to do so in future. This is another reason for the price increase post a stock split.

Share Buyback

Scenario –

1. On 05-JUN-2014, Board of directors of a large company *Super Furnishings*[28] announced that they are going to buy back **20%** of outstanding shares from the market.

2. The total outstanding shares in the market of *Super Furnishings* was **20 crore shares**.

---

[28] Fictitious company

3. The share buyback is at **Rs.38**. Until the day before this announcement was made, the shares of the company was trading at **Rs.35**.

Explanation –

1. Share buyback is the repurchase of outstanding shares by a company in order to reduce the number of shares on the market.
2. Companies will buy back shares either to increase the value of shares still available (reducing supply), or to eliminate any threats by shareholders who may be looking for a controlling stake[29].
3. Earnings per Share (EPS) of the company tend to increase post buyback because the total outstanding shares decrease consequent to buyback. This may also be a goal for share buyback. An increase in company shares (done through rights and bonus shares) can dilute the EPS to the shareholder when earnings fall or are not in line with street[30] expectations.
4. Share buyback is normally done at a premium to the market price. In this case there is Rs.3 premium to the market traded price which acts as an incentive to the current shareholders to part with their shares and sell it back to the company.

---

[29] This can be verified by a report published by the company called **Shareholding Pattern** report.

[30] Share market expectation is also sometimes referred to as Street expectation – In India the share market is at Dalal Street in Mumbai

Spot Buy Order (Market Price / Spot Price)

Scenario – I place an order to buy **20 shares** of Canara Bank at 10:30 AM on a Tuesday morning of a trading day at market price of **Rs.400** per share. The order is executed immediately.

Explanation –

1. This is a BUY transaction.
2. A transaction where one places an order at the current market price trending in the market is called **SPOT** order.
3. The order gets executed at a price that is being quoted in the market at the time it is placed. My bank account is debited by this amount plus the transaction and brokerage costs. In this case my account will be debited by about Rs.8,010 (assuming a brokerage of 0.1% and standard transaction taxes).
4. **20 shares** of Canara Bank will be credited to my account on Thursday of the same week.
5. Corresponding SPOT SELL order will be exactly the same except for the fact that it will be a SELL instead of a BUY.

Limit Buy Order

Scenario – I place an order to buy **100 shares** of Ashok Leyland at 9:45 AM on a Monday morning of a trading day. I place an order to buy the share only at a price of

Rs.48. I see that the share is trading at **Rs.49** in the market when I place the order.

Explanation –

1. This is a BUY transaction.
2. A transaction where one places an order at the certain predefined price level is called **LIMIT** order.
3. This BUY order will only get executed if the price of Ashok Leyland stock comes to exactly **Rs.48** as desired.
4. If the price of the Ashok Leyland does not reach **Rs.48** during the entire Monday on that day until 3:30 PM, then the order expires and no BUY happens on that day.
5. However, if the price does reach Rs.48 even for a fraction of a second on Monday, the order will be executed and **100 shares of Ashok Leyland** will be credited to the Demat account on Wednesday of the same week.
6. Corresponding **LIMIT SELL** order will be exactly the same except for the fact that it will be a SELL instead of a BUY.

Bulk Deals

Scenario – An ace investor in the stock market, on a single day, through a single client account, purchased **1 crore shares** of a company that amounted to a **1% stake** in the company. The broker, who facilitated this trade, provided this detail to the stock exchange on the same day.

Explanation –

1. If anyone in the stock market, during the day, purchases or sells a large number of shares which is equivalent to more than **0.5%** of the company's equity shares, then it is called bulk deal.

2. Each day, stock exchanges publish all the bulk deals of the previous trading day.

3. Bulk deals sometimes may act as a trigger for upward or downward price moves. It is an investment cue for other investors. But there is no guarantee that the price moves will happen just because of the bulk deals.

4. If a famed investor invests takes a stake in a company then it signals to the market that there is something worthwhile investing in the company and the prices may shoot up.

5. On the other hand, if an investor sells a large stake in a company on a single day, then the signal to other investors is that, not all is well with the company and so they tend to sell the shares thereby dropping the prices.

Block Deals

Scenario – A large mutual fund and a foreign institutional investor agree to trade shares worth Rs.20 crore on a single day. The stock price was agreed to be at a 1% discount to the previous day's closing price. They execute the trade in the stipulated time window in the stock market.

Explanation –

1. A deal that happens between two parties with mutual agreement to trade shares at a price is called a **block deal**.
2. Stock exchanges set a **35-minute** separate time window to allow for block deals.
3. The minimum threshold for a block deal is Rs.5 crore or 500,000 shares whichever is lower.
4. Retail investors cannot participate in block deals. It is only done by institutional investors.

Intraday trade

Scenario –

1. I place an order to **BUY 100 shares** of Chambal Fertilizers at 10 AM on a Thursday morning of a trading day at market price of **Rs.55 per share**. The order executes immediately.
2. At 1:00 PM, Chambal Fertilizers is trading at **Rs.59.5 per share**. I decide that I will sell the share because I'm making a profit on the transaction.
3. I place a **SELL** order to sell 100 shares of Chambal Fertilizers at market price. The sell transaction also executes at **Rs.59.5 per share**. My gross profit on this trade is **Rs.450.** {(59.5-55)*100}. This amount will be credited to my account on Monday next week.

Explanation –

1. This is a paired BUY-SELL transaction executed on the same day. This type of transaction is called INTRADAY trade. Also note that I bought and sold the same number of shares (100 shares in this case). So net-net I bought at **Rs.55** and then sold at **Rs.59.5** pocketing **Rs.450** on the trade.

2. The process of BUYING and SELLING the same quantity of stock on the same day is called **square-off trade or squaring off.**

3. Note that this is a very risky trading strategy as there is no guarantee that the price of the stock will increase. It may as well go below 55 and then you will be incurring loss.

4. To reiterate, if any BUY and SELL transaction of the same security (stock) is done on a single trading day (i.e. between 9:30 AM and 3:30 PM) then it is called as an INTRA-DAY trade.

Short-Selling

Scenario –

1. On Tuesday, I read a news article that a certain company called SPICY[31] is going through a crisis. On that day I think that SPICY share prices will fall because of the bad press it has got.

2. I do not have SPICY shares with me.

---

[31] A fictitious company

3. At 9:15 AM as soon as the market opens I SELL **1000 shares** of SPICY at Rs.17.50 market price.

4. As per my thinking, SPICY share prices begin to fall as there is more bad-news on that day about the company making news headlines. The share-prices fall to **Rs.15** at about 1:30 PM.

5. I decide that I will **BUY 1000 shares** of SPICY at Rs.15 and square-off the trade.

6. I place a **BUY** order for **1000 shares** of SPICY at Rs.15 market price. The trade is executed.

Explanation –

1. What's going on here? Firstly, I sold the shares I did not have at a higher price and then bought the same quantity of shares at a lower price. In the process I have managed to make money. I made **(17.5-15) *1000 = Rs.2,500** on the trade.

2. This process is called **SHORT-SELLING**[32]. You will observe that even though the share prices dropped I made a profit from the trade. I have reversed the BUY and SELL transactions by selling first and then buying at a lower price thus making a profit even in a downward price move.

3. Needless to say, this is a highly risky trading strategy and you may as well end up losing money on a not-so-lucky day. Generally, only professional traders with lots of experience engage in short-selling. It is not a recommended strategy for beginners and investors.

---

[32] This is also called by various names such as shorting or going short

4. Another important aspect is that share prices are sensitive to news and customer sentiment. Positive news about a company generally evokes lots of enthusiasm about a stock and stock prices can improve. Conversely, negative news will evoke lot of negative sentiment about the stock and the prices may begin to fall. But this is just a rule-of-thumb. Understanding markets is an art and there are no cast-in-stone perfect theories around how market may behave in short or long term.

Stop Loss

Scenario – Let's go through the same example of SPICY and consider the reverse scenario.

1. At 9:15 AM as the market opens I **SELL 1000 shares** of SPICY for **Rs.17.50** market price as I have read numerous articles about the impending bad news about the company's labor issue.
2. Things do not go as per plan and SPICY share prices begin to rise as the company issues a press statement that a solution has been found to the existing problem. I place a STOP-LOSS COVER BUY order at **Rs.20**
3. The share is trading at **Rs.20** at about 1:30 PM. My **STOP-LOSS COVER BUY** order gets executed.

Explanation –

1. Things did not go as per my plan and hence I ended up making a loss in this trade. Net-net I

bought **1000 shares** @ **Rs.20** and sold it at **Rs.17.5** thus making a loss of **Rs.2,500.**

2. You should always be cognizant of the fact that things might not go as per plan in the stock market. You may incur losses from time to time. But it is important to minimize risk.

3. **STOP-LOSS** is one such risk minimization strategy. It is always recommended to place a cover order just to ensure that you don't lose too much money than you can afford to.

4. **NEAT** software and other software applications allow the trader to place **COVER ORDERS** for **INTRADAY** trades. **COVER ORDERS** are nothing but **LIMIT** orders.

5. In the event of an absence of the COVER ORDER i.e. if the position is not squared-off, the shares need to be purchased in auction subsequently by the broker and the price difference has to be borne by the short-seller. Some brokers, however, choose to square-off all open positions at **3:15 PM** (15 minutes before stock market closes for the day) at whatever the market price is at that point in time. The highly recommended practice is to always have cover orders to square-off positions for intra-day positions.

6. To reiterate, this is an extremely risky trading strategy and you may as well end up losing money on a not-so-lucky day. Generally, only professional traders with lots of experience engage in short-selling. It is not a recommended strategy for beginners and investors.

Upper and Lower Circuit

Scenario –

1. On a particular day, a stock of a company named Deepak Nitrite rose from **Rs.77** to **Rs.92.4. An UPPER CIRCUIT price** was hit on the stock.

2. On another day another stock trading at Rs.500 dropped to Rs.450. A **LOWER CIRCUIT price** was hit on the stock.

Explanation –

1. Both stock indices and stocks have been set with CIRCUIT FILTERS for both **UPPER** and **LOWER** price moves.

2. UPPER CIRCUIT filters are set at levels of +5%, +10%, +20%. The level set varies from one stock to another. Some of the stocks will have +5% filters, some +10% filter and some with +20%.

3. In the first scenario above, the stock Deepak Nitrite rose from Rs.77 to 92.4 which is 20% increase. As Deepak Nitrite has a **UPPER CIRCUIT** level set at 20%, the stock is said to have hit the **UPPER CIRCUIT**. All subsequent transactions will have to happen at that price for the rest of the day once it hits the **UPPER CIRCUIT**. It is the closing price of the day for that stock.

4. **LOWER CIRCUIT** filters are set at levels of -5%, -10%, -20%. The level set varies from one stock to another. Some of the stocks will have -5% filters, some -10% filter and some with -20%.

5. In the second scenario, the stock drops from Rs.500 to Rs.450 which is a 10% drop (or -10%). The **LOWER CIRCUIT** level set on the stock being **-10%** makes it hit the **LOWER CIRCUIT** filter. All subsequent trades can only happen at that price point for the rest of the day once it hits the **LOWER CIRCUIT**. It is the closing price of the day for that stock.

6. One may ask as to why this phenomenon occurs. If you think about it the stock market is a place where buyers meets sellers and they trade at a given price point. This is a classic case of Demand-Supply economics!!

    a. Imagine a scenario when there is lots of good news about the company Deepak Nitrite and people are very positive about it.

    b. The existing shareholders of Deepak Nitrite think that the price of Deepak Nitrite will move higher from the current levels.

    c. There are other investors in the market who want to buy the stock of Deepak Nitrite because they think that it will offer good profits for them as the company is doing well and has lots of good news around it.

    d. The buyers want to buy the stock even for a higher price. Hence there is lot of demand for the stock Deepak Nitrite. However, the sellers do not want to sell the stock. Hence there is lack of supply of Deepak Nitrite shares.

    e. Logically, the price of the **stock rises** as demand increases and more and more people want to purchase it but are not able to because of lack of sellers.

  f.   To prevent any misuse of this situation, the regulator of the stock market has placed a UPPER circuit filter on each and every stock and index traded in the market.

7.   The exactly same reasoning can be done for LOWER CIRCUIT filters. Can you try working out the reason how that may occur? **[Hint: High Supply, Low Demand]**

Depositary Receipts (DR)

Scenario – *Retail Enterprises* believes that as a company its brand is extremely well known. It now wants to raise foreign capital by getting it listed in other stock exchanges internationally for instance in US and Europe.

1.   *Retail Enterprises* issues a Depositary Receipt issue in US Stock exchange after necessary formalities with US stock exchange.

2.   *Retail Enterprises* hopes to raise a capital of $10M from the depositary receipt issue.

3.   *Retail Enterprises* approaches a depositary bank registered with SEBI in India and transfers the shares.

4.   The depositary bank connects with the custodian bank in the foreign country and issues depositary receipts certificates.

5.   The depositary receipts certificates are issued by the custodian bank in the foreign country

through the US stock exchange and are priced in US dollars.

6. Dividends to depositary certificates are paid out in US dollars

Explanation – Depositary receipts is a negotiable financial instrument which is used to raise foreign capital for a company. In this case, *Retail Enterprises* plans to raise capital from US markets. For an US market investor, this represents investment in a foreign listed stock but through a simpler process of investing in an instrument that is locally available. These instruments are called **ADR**s (American Depositary Receipts) as they are issued in the US stock market. Typically, one ADR certificate will be equivalent to X number of shares. (X can be 5, 10 and so on).

If a European bank issues **DR**, then they are called European depositary receipts **(EDRs)** and if other banks issue them it is called Global depositary receipts (GDRs).

India being a growing capital market has seen lot of foreign institutional money flowing in the recent decades. A lot of international companies have shown interest in raising capital from Indian capital markets given the growth the Indian capital markets have witnessed lately. To facilitate a US company (or an international company) to raise capital from Indian capital markets, SEBI has launched Indian Depository Receipts (IDRs). IDRs will enable a foreign company to issue certificates and raise capital from Indian capital market. One can refer to a detailed PWC white-paper on IDRs[33] for more details on the product.

Market Sentiment

Scenario – One will always hear stock market analysts talk about the following on a very frequent basis.

1. The market sentiment has been extremely good and hence we are seeing increased market participation from all segments because of budgetary expectations and this is the reason for the 330 points rise in SENSEX today.

2. Today the markets tanked by 200 points mainly because of weak market sentiment on inflation fears and unemployment concerns coupled with weak industrial output data for the month of June.

Explanation – Market sentiment is an aggregate of all emotions and feelings of the market participants about the market and the economy. Investor (Behavioral) Psychology and behavioral finance are the academic disciplines which study how emotions work in markets. Unfortunately, market sentiment, being a qualitative measure, cannot be easily assigned a numerical scale. All that can be said is if the market sentiment was strong (upbeat, bullish) or weak (bearish). The market sentiment manifests itself in the actions undertaken thereon by the investor.

---

[33] https://www.pwc.in/assets/pdfs/Publications-2010/ Indian Depository reciept.pdf from PricewaterhouseCoopers (PWC), one of the Big Four accounting firms in the world

Fear, anxiety and greed are the common traits of human beings. Overcoming such emotions is a must for every winning trade. Confidence based on solid research, helps overcoming emotional trading decisions. However, real success in trading comes with discipline and experience. Hurried decisions costs investors more than ignorance.

Profit Booking and Correction

Scenario – An analyst report of stock market performance for the past two days in a newspaper stated as follows:

"After hitting life time highs earlier this week, both SENSEX and NIFTY saw a decline of 450 and 143 points respectively mainly due to profit-booking by both institutional and retail investors."

Explanation – If you follow the market reports in newspapers and websites, it is highly probable that you might have heard the term **profit booking**. Every investor in the market is in there only to realize profits! Profit realization is when you actually get the money credited in your account.

1. Say an investor has invested Rs.50,000 in a company by purchasing 1,000 shares at Rs.50 apiece.
2. The current stock price is Rs.65.
3. The investor rationale tells him that he needs to realize profits. He sells shares worth Rs.15,000 as his total profit is Rs.65,000 – Rs.50,000 =

    Rs.15,000. This is nearly equivalent to 230 shares that he needs to sell.

4. Rs.15,000 is the realized profit. He still has (1000-230) = **770 shares**.

5. There may be many such investors, who think alike. When many investors think that it is the right time to realize partial or complete profits, they begin to sell. This brings down the price as there is lot of supply of shares in the market.

6. The market sentiment is then known to be a **sellers' market[34]**.

7. A sellers' market occurs typically when there is a long bull run in the market.

8. This phenomenon of price drop across most of the stocks that lead to a drop in the main stock indices SENSEX and NIFTY is called **correction[35]**.

Insider Trading

Scenario – *Retail Enterprises* has directors in the company and other senior leadership who are in the know of the company strategy and a very large deal that they have made which only a few of the company management is privy to. As they are aware of this non-public strategy or information of the company, they invest in the stock of the company (*Retail Enterprises*) in the open market and get

---

[34] The opposite is buyers' market. Can you deduce when does a buyers' market situation occur?

[35] This is also called price correction. A correction that occurs for a small period of time is called short term correction and a longer term downtrend is called a long term correction.

profits based on such undisclosed company information which an average investor is unaware of.

Explanation –

1. This practice of trading with access to unpublished, company specific price sensitive information by connected persons are deemed to be illegal by SEBI guidelines and is known as **Insider Trading**.

2. SEBI has defined **connected persons** as all persons and their immediate relatives with a contractual fiduciary (trustees) or employment relationship with the company. This new regulation strengthens the legal and enforcement framework.

3. The onus of proving that they were not in possession of the price sensitive information lies with the person concerned.

4. Central idea of all these measures and legal enforcements are to establish the investor confidence and protect his interest to ensure continued capital investments. Investor is cardinal to the success of capital markets.

Tapering (Fed Tapering)

Central banks (RBI in India, Federal Reserve in US) play an important role in policy making and implementation to propel growth. It is a balancing act between short term improvements in the economy and long term expectations. We have seen that RBI or government securities are virtually risk free bonds as they is negligible (almost zero) default risk. This is the reason why the interest rates are low and are called risk-free interest rates. One of the techniques employed by the central banks is to start to purchase assets with long term maturities to lower the higher long term interest rates. Federal Reserve in US adopted this measure of buying long term mortgage assets during 2007 financial crisis. This brought down the long term interest rates as the financial institutions were now encouraged to lend money. This was called QE (Quantitative Easing). Tapering means, the gradual lowering of amount of assets purchased by Fed each month by looking at stability of macro-economic variables such as inflation and unemployment. As Federal Reserve announced this in 2013, this term is also known as **Fed Tapering**.

Freak Trades

Scenario –

1. In 2010, shares of Reliance industries crashed 20% on execution of a large sell order at a very low price entered wrongly during order placement.
2. On Oct 5, 2012, Nifty hit lower circuits as SPOT prices dropped by 900 points to end at **4,888** traced to an erroneous order placed by a large trader. Indian markets then recovered after this flash crash with normal trading resuming.

Explanation –

1. These are examples of erroneous trades that happen during trading either by systemic failure or a user input error. These are called **Freak Trades**.

2. Imagine that I want to sell 100 shares of a company trading at Rs.150. I try and place a limit SELL order as I want to ensure I sell at 150. I hurriedly place the order. Instead of entering 100 shares, I entered 100000 and instead of Rs.150 limit I enter Rs.15 and process the order. If there are no checks and balances to user input, this large sell order will completely skew the market prices of the stock and the prices will crash. It again relates to Demand-Supply mechanics of price. For instance, if a retailer quotes an expensive television at Rs.5,000 instead of Rs.50,000 erroneously, then suddenly he will have too many orders for the TV because the prices are the lowest among all sellers!!

3. SEBI has laid down clear guidelines to stock exchanges to have necessary checks in place to avoid **freak trades**.

4. Freak trades are rare, but when they happen, it causes lot of churn in the market.

CHAPTER IX

Other Capital Markets And Products

We have until now, seen stock markets in some detail. Stock markets deal with buying and selling of stocks of companies. This is only a part of the capital market. Some additional markets and products that you need to be aware of are briefed in this chapter.

FOREX MARKETS (FX or Foreign Exchange Markets)

Forex markets deals with foreign exchange trading. The participants of this market are able to buy, sell, exchange, and speculate on international currencies. Primary participants in currency markets are banks, commercial companies, central banks, investment management firms, hedge funds and retail forex brokers and investors. Forex markets are the largest financial markets in the world processing trillions of dollars' worth of transactions each day.

The foreign exchange markets is not dominated by a single market exchange, but involves a global network of computers and brokers from around the world. Central banks use their massive buying and selling capabilities to alter exchange rates through their open market activities and in many cases will do so with both profit and policy reasons in mind.

COMMODITY MARKETS

Commodity markets are a physical or virtual marketplace for buying, selling and trading raw or primary products. For investors' purposes there are currently about 50 major commodity markets worldwide that facilitate investors trade in nearly 100 primary commodities. Commodity markets in India are regulated by **Forward Markets Commission (FMC)** which was set up in 1953.

There are numerous ways to invest in commodities. An investor can purchase stock in corporations whose business relies on commodities prices, or purchase mutual funds, index funds or exchange-traded funds (ETFs) that have a focus on commodities-related companies. The most direct way of investing in commodities is by buying into a futures contract.

Commodities are split into two types

a. **Hard commodities** – typically natural resources that must be mined (gold, silver, rubber, oil etc).
b. **Soft commodities** – agricultural products or livestock (potato, wheat, coffee, sugar, soyabeans etc).

Another way of classifying commodities is:

    a. **Agricultural commodities** (Agri)
    b. **Non-Agricultural commodities** (Non-Agri)

In India there are two important commodity exchanges:

    1. **MCX** – Multi Commodity Exchange
    2. **NCDEX** – National Commodity and Derivatives Exchange

DERIVATIVES MARKETS

This is the market consisting of financial derivatives like futures contracts and options. These are called derivatives because these are derived from other form of assets. Derivative is a contract between two or more parties. The price of the derivative is determined by the fluctuations in the underlying asset. Commonly, underlying assets include stocks, bonds, commodities, currencies, interest rates and market indexes. Derivatives are generally used as an instrument to hedge risk but can also be used for speculative purposes.

Most common types of derivatives are

    1. *Forward contracts*
    2. *Future contracts*
    3. *Options*
    4. *Swaps*

CHAPTER X

Trend Determination Methods

Technical Analysis and Fundamental Analysis

We have until now, seen how stock markets operate and how to go about getting started with being an investor in the stock markets. The primary idea of investing is to get good return on investment and grow wealth. Ideally, every investor will want to buy at low prices and sell at high prices earning a good return. Naturally, the question that is asked is "*How does one determine the right candidate/ avenue to invest? Does one invest in Stock A or Stock B or in GOLD or in DEBT funds*" The answer to this question is not straightforward. The answer is dependent on the risk taking potential[36] of the individual and the window of time the investor wants to remain invested before he/she expects positive returns to hit their accounts. Additionally, a careful examination of the potential areas

---

[36] Risk taking potential is the extent of risk that an investor or company is willing to live with

of opportunity where the returns can be good forms the basis of determining where to invest. This careful examination methodology of evaluating financial assets has evolved over time into two broad branches. They are:

1. **Fundamental Analysis** – This method of analysis involves analyzing the financial statements of the asset (stock, debt instrument or anything that is subject to investment), its management, competitive advantages, its competitors and future potential. It also takes into account macroeconomic scenario, industrial production performance, earnings, employment, government policies and GDP. This analysis usually focuses more on the long term investment opportunities. The goal of this study is as discussed the following:

   a. To identify and recommend potential growth assets which can be invested in for good returns.

   b. To arrive at estimated guidance on business performance

2. **Technical Analysis**[37] – This method of analysis of a security deals with study of historical price data from the market to determine the future price trends. There is little or no emphasis on the specific company fundamentals. Technical analysis deals

---

[37] Neither fundamental nor technical analysis is 100% accurate. These are tools prescribed to determine price trends and investment opportunities but do not guarantee 100% accuracy. Nowadays there are automatic software applications that provide all technical and fundamental indicators of a company. One such software is provided by www.investarindia.com

with chart analysis of price and volume and a host of technical indicators that provide indication on trends. The people who specialize in this area are called *technical analysts*. Technical analysts believe that the historical performance of stocks and markets are indicators of future performance. This analysis usually focuses more on the short-term[38] investment opportunities.

Is summary, we perform technical analysis to answer two key questions:

a. **Where to invest?** Determine where to invest in the short-term

b. **What will be the future price trend?** Guidance on how the price trends are going to look like.

Technical Analysis Charts

In this section we take a very brief look at technical analysis charts.

Price Volume Charts

Consider the following basic price and volume[39] chart of a stock. This is a price trend of the stock from Dec-2013

---

[38] Short-term can be defined as an investment with a horizon of anywhere between 1 day to 1 year. Long term on the other hand is anywhere between 1 year to 5 years.

[39] In stock market terminology, volume means "***number of shares traded***"

to Dec-2014. The bottom half of the diagram indicates the volume of stocks traded.

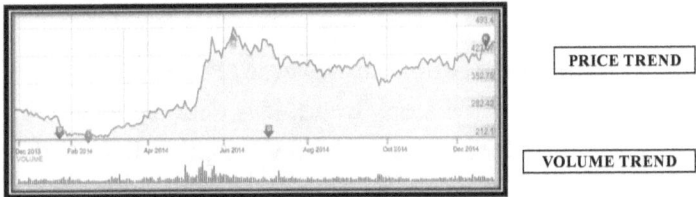

PRICE TREND

VOLUME TREND

Basic index chart of NIFTY index

Below is the chart indicating the index chart of NSE primary stock index called NIFTY as discussed earlier. This is a 6-month index trend.

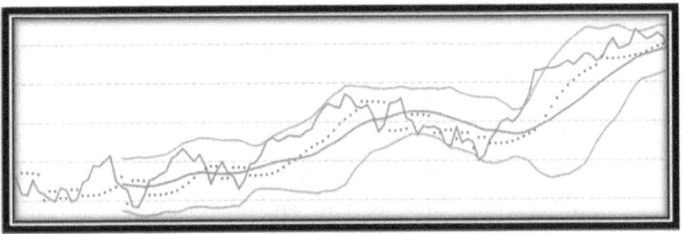

Technical analysis chart with key indicators[40]

Following is the chart with a few significant technical indicators[41] that are used as part of technical analysis. The few technical indicators shown in this chart below are:

---

[40] It is essential to develop a very good understanding of the technical indicators by studying them in detail and then apply them.

[41] For an excellent documentation of all chart patterns and technical indicators, their calculation methodology and use cases the reader can refer to http://stockcharts.com/school/doku.php?id=chart_school

1. **20 day Bollinger Bands** – These show the + **2 Standard Deviation** to **-2 Standard Deviation** bands of the **20-day** historical moving price averages.

2. **Parabolic Stop and Reverse (Parabolic SAR)** – Indicates the stock trend. It is denoted as a point (dot) either above or below the price line. If it is above the price line, the trend is negative and if the PSAR is below the price trend line then it indicates an uptrend.

3. **Average Directional Index (ADX)** – This technical indicator provides us the strength and direction of price movements. It is generally based on 14-day price moving averages. It has two components called +DI and –DI which are used to determine uptrend or downtrend of the stock. The value of ADX above 20 indicates that it is a strong trend.

4. **Moving Average Convergence Divergence (MACD)** – This is a price momentum oscillator and indicator. This is the most used oscillator to provide BUY or SELL signals for stocks.

5. **Relative Strength Index (RSI)** – A very popular technical indicator which signals overbought and oversold zones for a particular stock. It ranges from 0 to 100. Values of **RSI above 70** indicate **overbought** conditions in the market and **RSI below 30** indicate **oversold** conditions.

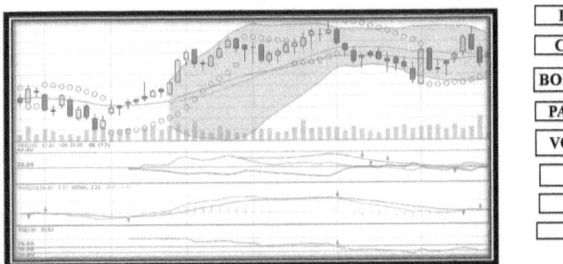

PRICE TREND
CANDLESTICK
BOLLINGER BAND
PARABOLIC SAR
VOLUME TREND
ADX
MACD
RSI

Commodity technical charts

Exactly same methodologies of technical analysis to stock can be readily applied to commodities as well. Actually, commodity markets are way older than the stock markets and some of the technical analysis methods started by studying commodities and were then adapted to stock trading!! We will now look at sample technical charts for a few commodities. Interested reader can consult the websites listed in the appendices to gain further knowledge.

GOLD

Below is the technical chart for GOLD. It is a 3 month trend chart overlayed with moving averages. The trend is that of price and volume and the technical indicators that are tracked are RSI and MACD.

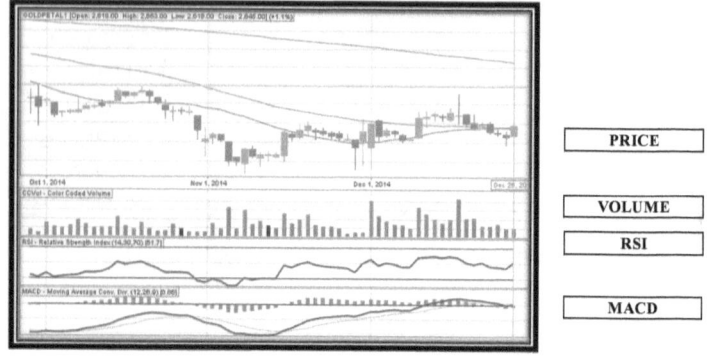

COTTON

Below is the technical chart for COTTON. It is a 3-month trend chart overlayed with moving averages. The trend is that of price and volume and the technical indicators that are tracked are RSI and MACD.

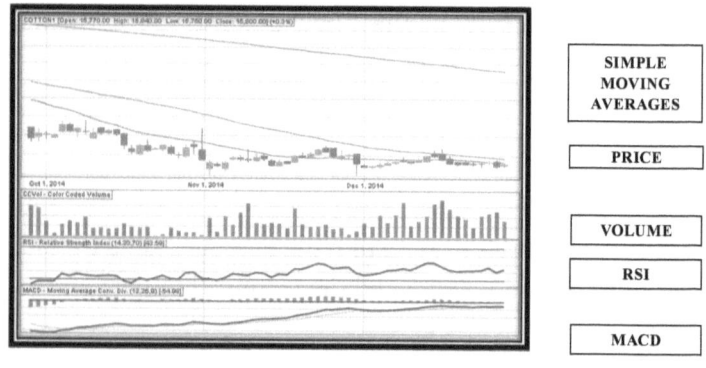

Concept of Moving Averages

Most of the technical indicators are designed using a concept called **moving averages**. The stock market price patterns are studied using this technique of moving averages. The below example defines and illustrates the calculations of moving averages.

Scenario –

Retail Enterprises listed on the stock market and an analyst tracks the closing prices of the stock each day. Below table shows the prices of *Retail Enterprises* for the first 20 days of its debut in the stock market.

Daily share prices of *Retail Enterprises* since listing			
Day	Closing Price (Rs)	3-day Moving Average (3DMA)	5-Day Moving Average (5DMA)
1	18		
2	16		
3	14	16.0	
4	20	16.7	
5	19	17.7	17.4
6	17	18.7	17.2
7	21	19.0	18.2
8	20	19.3	19.4
9	26	22.3	20.6
10	24	23.3	21.6
11	21	23.7	22.4
12	15	20.0	21.2
13	22	19.3	21.6
14	28	21.7	22
15	24	24.7	22
16	29	27.0	23.6
17	32	28.3	27
18	27	29.3	28
19	27	28.7	27.8
20	35	29.7	30

Based on the closing price, the analyst tries to calculate the 3 day moving average of the price. 3 day moving average for day 3 is defined as follows:

3DMA for Day 3 = [Closing Price of Day 1 + Closing Price of Day 2 + Closing Price of Day 3] / 3

So, for Day 3, 3DMA = [Rs.18 + Rs.16 + Rs.14] / 3 = Rs.**16**

Putting this in words, all we have done is calculated the average price of the stock based on closing prices for the past 3 days. You will see that the 3 day moving average can only be calculated once we have stock prices for at least 3 days. That is the reason why there is no 3DMA defined after Day 1 and Day 2.

For the next day, i.e. day 4, the 3 DMA will be

3DMA for Day 4 = [Closing Price of Day 2 + Closing Price of Day 3 + Closing Price of Day 4] / 3

You observe that we have considered closing prices of day 2 through day 4 and have dropped the prices on day 1 to calculate 3 DMA for day 4. So, 3 DMA for any day will be the average closing price of preceding 3 days.

Similarly, 5 day moving average (or 5DMA) is calculated as:

5DMA for day 5 = [Sum of closing prices of Day 1 through Day 5] / 5

The same set of calculations can be done to work out the 5DMA for all days as shown.

The analyst also plots these numbers on a graph and it looks something like this:

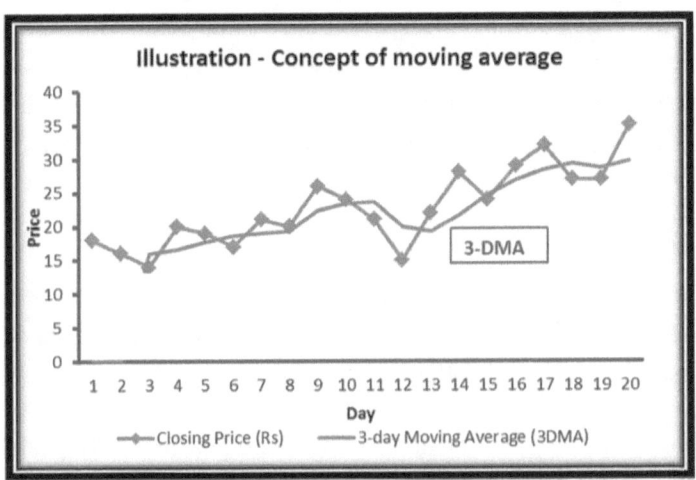

Explanation –

Observe the diagram above. It plots the daily closing prices of *Retail Enterprises*. It also tracks the daily 3DMA. One can observe that while the daily closing price line has lot of zig-zag[42] movements, the 3DMA line is a little smoother. The 3 DMA line smoothens the prices for 3 consecutive rolling days. It can be used to indicate the trend of the stock which might be a little difficult if we use the daily closing price chart alone.

On similar lines, we can construct 5DMA, 9DMA, 10DMA, 14DMA, 26DMA, 50DMA, 200DMA and so on.

200DMA is a 200 day moving average which means that every point on the 200 DMA line has been calculated by using last 200 days closing prices. This means that it is a

---

[42] This is also called as see-saw as the price movements resemble the see saw blade edges.

long term trend detector and that's exactly how it is used. 50 DMA is also used as a short term trend detector among other techniques. Every point used to construct 50DMA is an average price point using last 50 days closing prices of the underlying stock or asset.

Most of the technical indicators constructed use 14DMA and 26DMA for short term trading signals. For instance, MACD which is a very popular short term trend indicator uses 26DMA and 14DMA to generate signals.

Needless to say, these moving averages are extremely important in almost all technical indicator calculations and are pivotal to determine trends.

There are many ways in which a moving average can be constructed. Important ones are:

1. Simple moving average (SMA)
2. Exponential moving average (EMA)

SMA is what was discussed in the example above. It is a mathematical average of the last n days of the n-Day Moving Average.

EMA is a little more complicated moving average. This is computed by providing weights to each closing price point. The latest prices are given more weightage compared to older prices. By doing this adjustment, one can determine the short term trends better than the simple moving average.

Fundamental Analysis with key indicators

In fundamental analysis of a company, as discussed earlier, one looks closely at the financial statements. Below is an example of a typical analysis of a company.

Illustration 1 – A Chemical major

Given below are key financial ratios of a large chemical company, and its historical financial indicators.

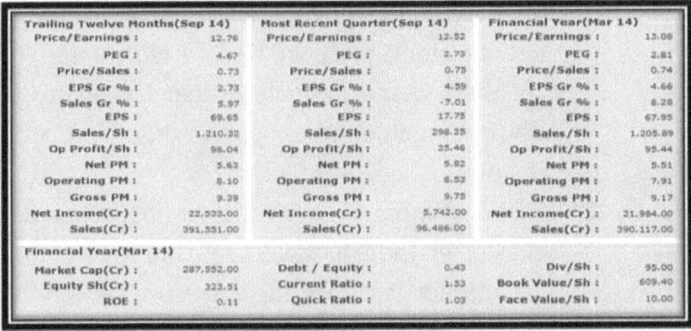

Trailing Twelve Months(Sep 14)		Most Recent Quarter(Sep 14)		Financial Year(Mar 14)	
Price/Earnings :	12.76	Price/Earnings :	12.52	Price/Earnings :	13.08
PEG :	4.67	PEG :	2.73	PEG :	2.81
Price/Sales :	0.73	Price/Sales :	0.73	Price/Sales :	0.74
EPS Gr % :	2.73	EPS Gr % :	4.59	EPS Gr % :	4.66
Sales Gr % :	5.97	Sales Gr % :	-7.01	Sales Gr % :	6.28
EPS :	69.65	EPS :	17.75	EPS :	67.95
Sales/Sh :	1,210.32	Sales/Sh :	298.25	Sales/Sh :	1,205.89
Op Profit/Sh :	98.04	Op Profit/Sh :	25.46	Op Profit/Sh :	95.44
Net PM :	5.63	Net PM :	5.82	Net PM :	5.51
Operating PM :	8.10	Operating PM :	6.53	Operating PM :	7.91
Gross PM :	9.39	Gross PM :	9.75	Gross PM :	9.17
Net Income(Cr) :	22,933.00	Net Income(Cr) :	5,742.00	Net Income(Cr) :	21,984.00
Sales(Cr) :	391,551.00	Sales(Cr) :	96,486.00	Sales(Cr) :	390,117.00
Financial Year(Mar 14)					
Market Cap(Cr) :	287,552.00	Debt / Equity :	0.43	Div/Sh :	95.00
Equity Sh(Cr) :	323.51	Current Ratio :	1.53	Book Value/Sh :	609.40
ROE :	0.11	Quick Ratio :	1.03	Face Value/Sh :	10.00

The key indicators used are:

1. **P/E (Price to Earnings) ratio** – This is perhaps the most important of all the fundamental performance ratios. It is easy, intuitive and comparable easily across all companies in the sector. It is defined as:

    P/E Ratio = [{Market Value per Share} / {Earnings per Share}]

P/E ratio indicates

    a. How much investors are willing to pay per rupee earned by the company. In this example the P/E of **the company** is 13 which imply that investors are willing to pay Rs.13 for every Rs.1 earned.

    b. P/E ratio is a definitive indicator of the value of the stock. For instance, if there are two companies in the same industry with similar growth rates – Company A with Stock price of Rs.10 with a P/E of 75 and another Company B with stock price of Rs.100 with a P/E of 20, then we can conclude that Company A stock is much more expensive than Company B stock.

    c. If the company has a higher P/E than the market or industry average, this means that the market is expecting big things over the next few months or years from the company and hence the willingness to invest at higher prices.

    d. A company with higher P/E ratio has the challenge to live to up the high expectations by substantially increasing its earnings else the stock prices will drop.

2. **EPS (Earnings Per Share)** – Earnings Per Share is the portion of a company's profit allocated to each outstanding share of common stock.

The formula to calculate EPS is:

Earnings Per Share = {Net Income}[43] / {Average Outstanding Shares}[44]

EPS is considered to be the single most important factor in determining a share's price.

3. **Debt to Equity Ratio (D/E)**[45] – This ratio is a measure of the company's financial leverage. It is calculated by dividing its total liabilities by shareholder equity. In simple terms it states how much of rupees is funded by Debt for every rupee funded by shareholders. In the above example we see that **the company** has Debt/Equity of **0.43** which implies that the company has a debt of **43 paisa** for every **rupee** invested by shareholder.

   a. If **D/E ratio** is 2, say, then it implies that **debt is twice the shareholder equity**. A higher D/E indicates that the company has lots of debts which in turn will affect the earnings because of financing cost (interest costs).

   b. There are a few variants to the way D/E calculated with respect to the numerator term **debt.** It is important to understand the basis of calculations before arriving at a conclusion.

---

[43] Numerator sometimes is also stated as {Net Income – Dividends on preferred stock} to ensure that the income is purely the one that is for the equity stockholders and does not include any payments reserved towards obligations to creditors of the company such as preferred stock dividend payouts.

[44] Average outstanding shares is calculated either as a weighted average number of shares outstanding over the reporting term or using the end of term number

[45] This ratio is also known as Risk, Gearing or Leverage.

i. Version 1 D/E – {Debt / Equity}

ii. Version 2 D/E – {Long-term Debt / Equity}

iii. Version 3 D/E – {Total Liabilities / Equity}

4. **Current Ratio**[46] – This ratio provides an idea of the company's ability to pay back its short-term liabilities (debt and payables) with its short-term[47] assets (cash, inventory, receivables). The higher the current ratio, the more capable the company is of paying its obligations.

$$\text{Current Ratio} = [\{\text{Current Assets}\} / \{\text{Current Liabilities}\}]$$

a. **Current ratio** is a good measure of the company's ability to turn its product into cash. Companies that have trouble getting paid on their receivables or have long inventory turnover can run into liquidity problems because of their inability to meet their obligations.

b. It is advisable to compare current ratios of same industry verticals.

c. Current ratio of **1.53** in the example above indicates that it is a healthy company which can meet its obligations through its current assets.

d. In general, **current ratio** between **1.5 and 3** is considered to be a healthy range.

---

[46] **Working Capital = {Current Assets – Current Liabilities}**

[47] Short-term indicates 12 months

5. **Quick Ratio (Acid Test Ratio or Liquid Ratio)** – This is similar to **current ratio** but does not include inventory. **Quick ratio** greater than **1** indicates a good liquidity position of the company. Quick ratio of **1.03** which indicates good liquidity.

Acid Test Ratio (Quick Ratio) = [{Current Assets – Inventory} / {Current Liabilities}]

6. **ROE (Return on Equity)[48]** – This is one of the most important fundamental ratio used to evaluate stocks. Return on Equity (ROE) is defined as:

ROE = {Net Income} / {Shareholders Equity}

   a. ROE is useful for comparing the profitability of a company to that of other firms in the same industry.
   b. ROE in the range of 15% and 20% are considered to be good.
   c. ROE of the chemical major for fiscal year 2014 is 0.11 or **11%.**

7. **Market Capitalization** – Market capitalization of the company is **Rs.2,87,552 crores.** It is calculated as the **{Total Outstanding Shares} * {Price of Stock}**

---

[48] DuPont Formula for ROE = ({Net Income}/ {Sales}) * ({Sales}/{Total Assets}) * ({Total Assets}/{Average Shareholder Equity}). The first term is **"Net Margin"**, the second is **"Asset Turnover"** and the third is **"Financial Leverage"**. Change to any one increases the ROE of the company.

8. **Dividend / Share (DPS)** – As discussed earlier, dividend is the profit share that is distributed among the shareholders.

Dividend Per Share = [{Total amount paid out in dividends} / {Total Outstanding[49] Shares}]

The company has a DPS of **95** which implies that it has paid out Rs.95 per share as dividends in financial year 2014.

9. **Book Value / Share** – Book value refers to the total amount a company would be worth if it liquidated its assets and paid all its liabilities. Book value can be calculated as follows:

Book Value = {Total Assets – Total Liabilities – Intangible Assets[50]}

Book Value per share = {Book Value} / {Total Number of Outstanding Shares}

Illustration 2 – Historical analysis through graphs

Another way to look at trends is to look the numbers graphically. This is particularly useful when you are studying a stock across many years. Let's consider the performance of various fundamental ratios and numbers of a fictitious company for the last 5 years.

---

[49] **Total Outstanding Shares** implies the total number of shares that are available for trade in the market

[50] Intagible assets include brand, patents

1. **Total Assets (rupees in crores) and Asset Turnover Ratio**

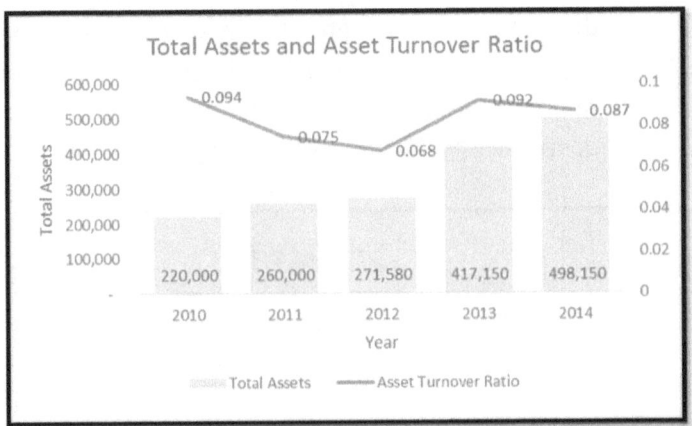

2. **Historical trend of Profit Before Tax (PBT) and Profit After Tax (PAT)** – We observe that the profits of the company have been on the downward trend since 2011.

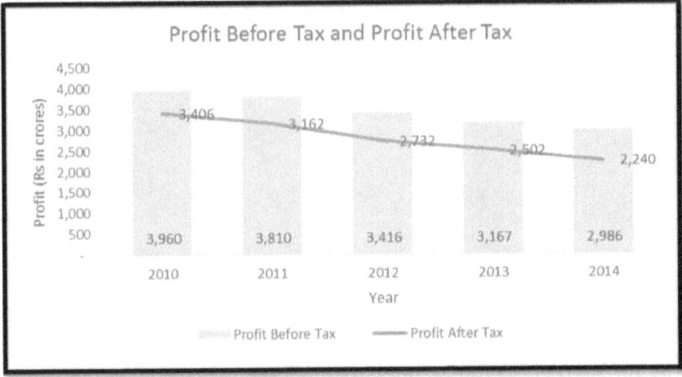

3. **Dividend paid compared with Net Profit** – We observe that though the Net profits have been trending downward for the company, it has paid dividends each year and the dividend percentages have progressively been largely consistent which might mean that they are wanting to have investor confidence by sharing profits each year as dividends.

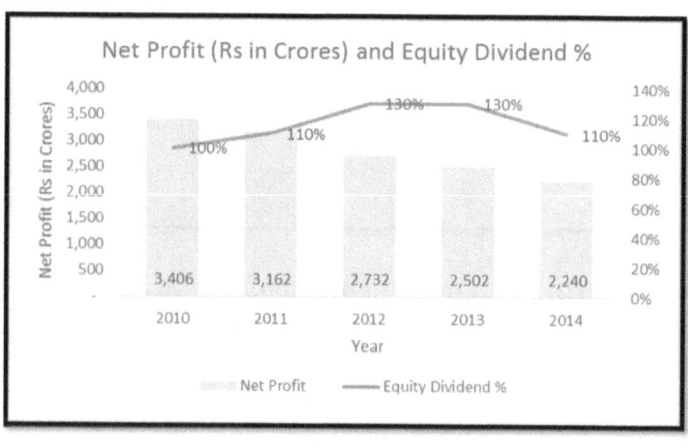

4. **Book Value Trend** – We observe that from fiscal 2010, the book value trend of the company is improving which implies that the total assets of the company have been improving.

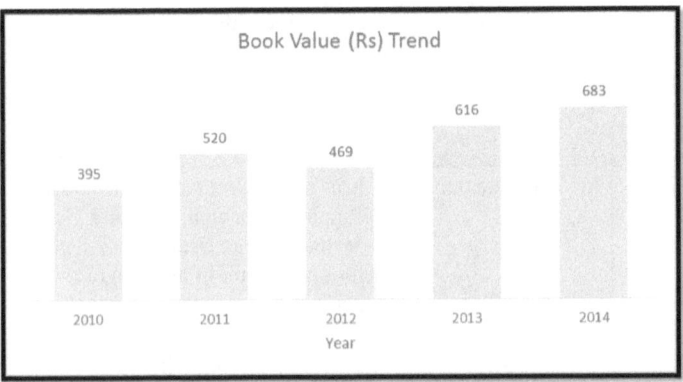

Book Value (Rs) Trend

Key Financial statements that aid fundamental analysis

The most important financial statements of a publicly listed company that are shared with everyone on a quarterly basis are:

- Balance Sheet
- Income statement
- Cash flow statement
- Shareholding Statement of a company

Sl No	Financial Statement	Utility to the investor
1	Balance Sheet	It provides a snapshot of company health. It fundamentally has assets, liabilities and capital of a business at a point in time. Investors can use this to assess: 1. Net worth of the company 2. Working capital position 3. Sustenance of operations 4. Assess health using various ratios
2	Income statement	Provides a summary of income and expenses of a company for a given period of time. Usually it is stated for one quarter (3 months) or a period of 12 months. Investors can use it to assess: 1. Operational health of the company 2. Profitability
3	Cash flow statement	Provides a summary of all cash flow transactions broken into broadly operational cash flows, investing cash flows and financial activities. Investors can use this to assess: 1. Free cash flow generated by the company 2. Company health
4	Shareholding statement	It provides the following information: a. Category of shareholders b. Number of shareholders c. Total number of shares d. Total % shareholding

CHAPTER XI

Fixed Income Securities

We discussed that owning shares (stocks, equity) is equivalent to owning a piece of a company that we have invested the shares in. We also discussed that another way of getting funding for business is to get it funded through loans.

Let us return to the example of *Retail Enterprises*. Suppose, the owners of Retail Enterprises, had decided to get the funding done by loans instead of going public, then what were the options they had? They had couple of options:

1. Bank loans (long term financing)
2. Company Deposits / Bonds – A loan instrument which promises the investor a fixed interest rate. The investors are creditors to the company for a set term defined in the contract.

You will observe a resemblance between **Bonds** and **Shares**. The primary difference between the two are that **shares** are a piece of ownership of the company whereas **bonds** or **company deposits** are a long term loan provided by the investor to the company at a promised interest rate that is either paid out quarterly or annually as per the contractual agreements. The security will have a maturity date when the company is obligated to return the outstanding principal amount to the investor, thus repaying the loan. As a creditor, the investor has a higher claim to the assets of the entity as compared to the shareholder but he does not have share in the profits. So a bond holder will neither get dividends issued by the company nor voting rights.

As they have a pre-defined fixed income, these financial instruments are called **Fixed Income Securities**. Fixed income securities, though long term instruments are freely tradable in open markets called Debt Markets.

Terminology of Bonds

Issuer

Scenario – Government of India issues a 5 year Infrastructure Taxable Bonds

Explanation –

1. Government of India is the issuer of this bond.
2. Fixed income securities can be issued by Central and State governments, Municipal Corporations, Govt. bodies or by private entities like financial institutions, banks and corporates provided they

    meet the statutory norms to issue those specific securities.

3.   Bonds issued can be taxable or non-taxable

Coupon or Interest rate

Scenario – Government of India issues a 5-year Infrastructure Taxable Bonds at an annual interest rate of 7.5% payable half-yearly.

Explanation –

1.   Annual interest promised by the Issuer is called the coupon rate or interest rate of the bond
2.   Interest is payable quarterly, semi-annually or annually.
3.   Interest payments can be taxed or can be tax free.
4.   In the above example 7.5% is the coupon rate and is payable every 6 months.
5.   Some bonds also have an interest re-investment option that can be availed where no interest will be paid out in the interim but will be reinvested and compounded and paid out only at maturity of the bond in one lump-sum payment.

Tenure/Maturity

Scenario – Retail Enterprises issues **7-year Bonds** at an annual interest rate of 10.5% payable half-yearly.

Explanation –

1. Tenure or Maturity of the bond is 7 years from the date it was bought.
2. The bond is offered during a window of time (typically the issue opens for 3 weeks and is closed after that). Investors are required to purchase the bonds within this time window of 3 weeks. These are called Close-Ended schemes.
3. Maturity periods less than a year are called Short Term instruments.

Face Value / Par Value

Scenario – Retail Enterprises issues **7-year Bonds** at an annual interest rate of 10.5% payable half-yearly at face value of Rs.1,000. Minimum investment is Rs.1000 and multiples of 1000 thereof.

Explanation –

1. Face value of the bond is the value of maturity of the bond. This is the amount the investor will get after 7 years per bond.
2. In this case, the investor will get the interest of 10.5% per annum for 7 years and then get the Rs.1000 back after 7 years.

Bond Yield

Scenario – Retail Enterprises issues **7-year Bonds** at an annual interest rate of 10.5% payable half-yearly at face value of Rs.1,000.

Explanation –

1. Bond Yield is the amount of return an investor will realize on the bond.
2. In this case, if an investor has invested Rs.1000 on the bond, he will get Rs.105 as the interest for one year. Yield is 105/1000 = 10.5% which is same as the Coupon rate. But if the bond price fell in the market to say Rs.900 then the Yield will be 105/900 = 11.67%.
3. Bond Yield and Bond Price are inversely related. As bond prices increase, bond yield decreases and vice-versa.
4. In a market where people want to go for safer instruments, bond prices will rise and yields will drop.

Debt Instruments

Fixed Deposits

This well-known financial instrument provided by banks is generally a fixed time window deposit wherein the bank pays a stipulated amount of interest (generally compound interest). The interest rates offered by fixed deposits are higher than the savings bank account deposits owing to the low liquidity of these investments. These funds internally are used a loans by the banks. The banks charge a higher rate of interest on the loans and fund the interest that is given to these fixed deposits. These are considered to be the safest instruments (almost risk-free). A few variants of the fixed deposits are:

1. **Recurring deposit (RDs)** – A pre-determined sum of money is deposited at a pre-defined interval (monthly, quarterly etc). The interest rates are calculated based on these payments depending on time value of money calculations.
2. **Flexi-fixed deposits** – These are instruments that combine the liquidity of savings bank accounts and the higher interest rates of fixed term deposits.

Company Deposits (CD)

Company deposits are fixed term, higher interest paying debt instruments issued by companies or NBFCs. These are used by companies to borrow large sum of money from a public group of investors (both individual and institutional). The higher interest of company deposits is because of higher risk associated with these deposits. Post maturity, the amounts with interest are returned by the company.

Fixed Maturity Plans (FMPs)

These are closed-ended debt funds with fixed maturity periods (typically 1, 3 and 5 years). The funds who release FMPs generally invest in government securities and company deposits. Interests on FMPs are taxed using indexation[51] and hence in times of high interest rates,

---

[51] Indexation is a technique to adjust income payments by means of a price index, so that the payments are adjusted for inflation.
Indexed purchase price = Purchase price * (CPI of current year/ CPI of year of purchase) where CPI is Consumer Price Index

the tax on interest is low unlike fixed deposits where the interest is taxed without indexation.

Commercial Paper

Commercial paper is a short-term (less than 270 days) debt instrument. This is used by companies to raise short term capital from the market. It is an unsecured[52] instrument.

Treasury Bills (T-Bills)

Treasury bills or T-Bills are short-term debt instruments used by Government of India to raise short-term capital. These are issued at discount to the face value as promissory notes.

DEBT MARKET SEGMENTS

Secondary debt markets are broadly classified into

1. Wholesale Debt Markets (WDM)
2. Retail Debt Markets (RDM)

Wholesale Debt Markets (WDM)

The primary investors in these markets are Banks, Financial Institutions, RBI and Insurance companies, Mutual Funds, Corporates and Foreign Institutional Investors (FIIs).

Following are the types of securities that are traded in WDMs.

---

[52] No collateral attached to the instrument

1. Government Bonds
2. State Government Bonds
3. Treasury Bills
4. State Enterprise Bonds
5. Financial Institutions
6. PSU Bonds
7. Bank Bonds
8. Corporate Debt
9. Supra Institutional Bonds
10. Local bodies
11. Mutual Fund

An example of the yield curve for a bond for month of Nov-2014 tracked daily. You see that the fall in yield across November signaling that the Bond prices are increasing.

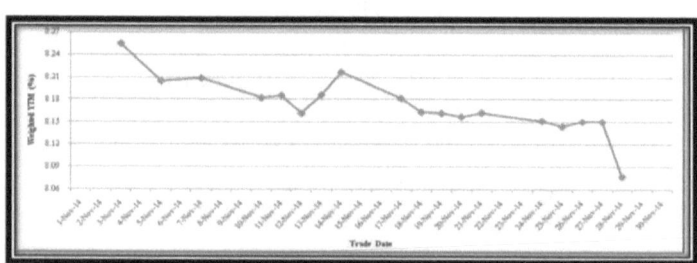

Typical example of bond listings in the market

COMPANY NAME ▼	LAST PRICE	CHANGE(%)	OPEN	HIGH	LOW	VOLUME	FACE VALUE
ECL Finance Series : N5	1,051.50	0.05%	1,051.50	1,051.50	1,051.50	85	1,000
ECL Finance Series : N4	1,120.00	1.80%	1,090.01	1,120.00	1,090.01	19	1,000
ECL Finance Series : N1	1,022.01	0.10%	1,024.00	1,024.00	1,022.01	88	1,000
Housing and Urban Development Corporation Series : N2	1,149.00	0.25%	1,146.00	1,149.00	1,146.00	2510	1,000
Housing and Urban Development Corporation Series : N5	1,095.00	-0.37%	1,085.00	1,085.00	1,095.00	700	1,000
Housing and Urban Development Corporation Series : N3	1,117.00	0.09%	1,116.00	1,118.00	1,116.00	3502	1,000
India Infoline Finance Series : N7	1,285.00	0.70%	1,270.00	1,285.00	1,270.00	60	1,000
India Infoline Finance Series : N5	1,053.04	0.29%	1,050.10	1,053.45	1,046.01	755	1,000
India Infoline Finance Series : N6	1,020.28	0.02%	1,021.30	1,023.62	1,019.25	1647	1,000

Retail Debt Markets (RDM)

The primary investors in these markets are:

1. Individual investors
2. Mutual Funds
3. Provident funds
4. Pension funds
5. Religious trusts and charitable organizations
6. State and district co-operative banks
7. Housing finance companies
8. NBFCs
9. Corporate treasuries
10. HUFs

CHAPTER XII

Mutual Funds

We have seen that making a smart investment decision is both a science and an art. This can get a little overwhelming and complicated for an average investor who has little knowledge about intricacies of the investment instruments. The need for an investment professional was seen a few decades ago and this discipline has since then seen lots of research and development. It has evolved as a specialized work-stream and is known by various names such as equity research, capital advisory, financial analytics, financial engineering, and technical analysis and so on.

One such important development has been the introduction of pooled investments that are managed professionally by an experienced fund manager who charges a nominal fee for providing the services. Popularly, these pooled investments are known as mutual funds.

Let's understand mutual funds through a simple hypothetical example.

Illustration of a mutual fund

Consider a small town with **100 people** who are interested to invest. One person, say, Mr.G arrives in this town. He knows a great deal about investing and has a vast experience in managing investments. He proposes the following plan:

1. Every people in town decide on a monthly instalment amount they wish to invest.
2. They pool in the money each month and give it to Mr.G
3. Mr. G then invests that money in the best available investment instrument by applying his decades of learning and experience.
4. Mr.G breaks the entire amount into two portions.

   a. He invests the first 50% of the amount in equity markets.
   b. He invests the rest of the amount in debt markets

5. Mr.G charges Rs.5 for every Rs.1000 he manages.
6. The people continue to pool in money each month and provide it Mr.G and he continues to invest the money.
7. Mr.G provides an investment account summary each month to all the 100 people in the town which indicates the amount of money that the individual has invested and the current value of the investment. He publishes a monthly report

which highlights the investments he has made and the Net Value of Assets.

8. Mr.G provides everyone an opportunity to withdraw his investment either fully or partly whenever the person thinks he/she wants his/her investment back.

This in essence is a **Mutual Fund**. It is a fund that is generated by pooling investments of a large group of people and is completely managed by person who is called Fund Manager[53]. Fund manager is a person who has a wealth of experience in investments. In our example above Mr.G is the fund manager. The fund is called "MUTUAL" as all of its returns, minus its expenses, are shared by the fund's investors.

Benefits of a mutual fund

There are a number of benefits of mutual funds:

1. **Professional management** – An average investor lacks adequate knowledge about capital markets and has limited resources. Hence the presence of a professional expert helps the investor with strategic best value investment decisions which will return superior returns compared to an average individual investor.

2. **Portfolio diversification** – Mutual funds invest money in a number of companies across various

---

[53] In real life, a fund manager will have an analyst team which does all the research work that is required to ensure attractive returns to the investments made

industrial sectors. This diversification reduces the overall risk of investments.

3. **Liquidity**[54] – Mutual funds are very liquid funds. Selling the units is really simple and fast.

4. **Convenience** – Mutual funds are a one stop shop to invest and helps reduce lot of time and effort for an average investor who has neither time nor patience to understand the nitty-gritty of capital markets and investments.

5. **Flexibility** – Mutual funds offer a whole host of investment products to suit the need of all risk-profile customers. They also provide options for systematic investment plans, systematic withdrawal plans and systematic transfer plans.

6. **Tax benefits** – Gains from mutual funds are tax exempt to a certain annual limit. Mutual funds also provide specific schemes which are eligible for tax exemptions. These mutual fund schemes are called ELSS (Equity Linked Saving Schemes). ELSS schemes generally have a 3 year lock-in period before which no withdrawal is permitted.

7. **Transparency** – Mutual funds release reports of their holdings to all investors and the market each month. In addition, they also provide customized reports to each investor clearly detailing total amount invested and the current market value of the investments.

8. **Stability to the stock market** – Mutual funds have very high amount of funds (commonly called as Corpus. Size of mutual funds are measured

---

[54] Liquidity means the ease of convertibility to cash

by a number called Assets Under Management commonly known as AUM) giving them the economies of scale by which they are flexible enough to absorb losses in short term and keep invested in the stock market with a long term in mind. This may not be possible for a single investor who can get into lot of financial difficulties because of a short term loss and can get discouraged from entering into the stock markets thus potentially losing out on the long term gains. Additionally, mutual funds increase liquidity in both money markets and capital markets.

9. **Research** – Mutual funds are well equipped with a team of professionals who spend their time in research on investment opportunities by studying and following the capital markets closely.

Structure of mutual fund

Following is a simplified structure of Mutual funds in India governed by SEBI.

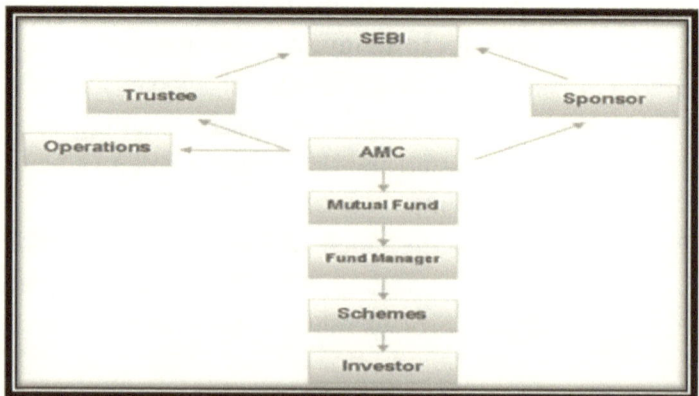

A Mutual fund is set up in the form of a trust, which has SPONSORS, TRUSTEES, AMC (Asset Management Company) and a Custodian. The Trust is established by a SPONSOR or more than one SPONSOR who is like a promoter of a company. The Trustees of the mutual fund hold its property for the benefit of the unit holders. The SEBI approved AMC, manages the funds by making investments in various types of securities. The custodian, registered with SEBI, holds the securities of various schemes of the fund in its custody. Trustees ensure compliance to SEBI regulations by the mutual fund.

Types of funds

A mutual fund house typically operates a number of funds (schemes) to cater to the various risk-profiles of investors. Each type of fund is headed by a manager called the fund manager. He is assisted by a team of investment professionals who provide him relevant decision support on his investment decisions. The investor is free to choose the fund house and the scheme he wants to invest in. Mutual fund houses also have a sales and marketing group of advisors who provide help and guidance to investors on best investment schemes of the fund house. Following diagram shows a brief on the various types of schemes that a typical mutual fund house offers.

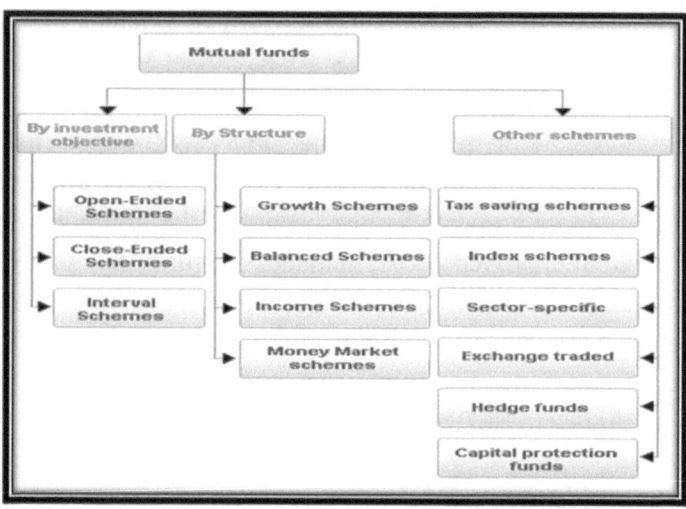

Type of MF scheme	Purpose	How do the MFs invest
Based on Investment objective		
Equity/Growth Schemes	For investors who are looking at long term growth opportunities and have slightly higher risk tolerance and higher risk appetite.	MF's of growth schemes invest a large share of their corpus in equity and related securities.
Balanced schemes	For investors looking for mixture of safety and growth with controlled risk.	Typically, fund managers of balanced funds have equal allocations in debt and equity instruments.
Debt/Income schemes	Targeted towards investors who are medium to low on risk tolerance	Fund managers of these funds invest a large amount of corpus in debt and related instruments.

Type of MF scheme	Purpose	How do the MFs invest
Money market schemes / Liquid funds	These are for investors who are looking at parking some additional funds for a short amount of time before they can decide on their long term goals. They need their funds to be secure but earn interest and be liquid.	These funds typically invest in T-Bills, CDs and other short term instruments that provide high liquidity, high safety and moderate returns.
Gilt funds	Targeted towards investors who are medium to low on risk tolerance	Funds invest exclusively in government securities. These are almost risk-free investments
Based on Maturity Period		
Open Ended Fund		Funds that can always be invested in.
Close ended fund		Funds that is open for a window of time. They have a fixed maturity period. They are listed in stock exchanges.
Interval fund		Have features of both closed and open ended funds combined. These funds can be traded in stock exchanges and are open for sale or redemption at pre-determined intervals at the prevailing NAV (Net Asset Value)

Type of MF scheme	Purpose	How do the MFs invest
Other schemes		
Tax Saving (ELSS) Funds	Investors looking for tax saving schemes to avail tax rebates and those who have high risk tolerance.	These funds invest primarily in equities.
Index Funds	Diversified portfolio seekers with lowest transaction costs.	These funds are not actively managed as they mimic the index definitions discussed earlier. They replicate the performance of the index that they are following. For instance, NIFTYBEES is an index ETF which replicates the performance of NIFTY.
Sector specific funds	Investors who are bullish on a sector (for instance realty sector) and want to invest in that sector chose sectoral funds. Investors need to be high risk tolerant.	Funds invest in the only the specific sectors as specified in the scheme information document. The performance of these funds is completely dependent on the sector performance. These are risky funds.

Net Asset Value (NAV)

Net Asset Value is the total asset value (net of expenses) per unit of the fund and is calculated by the fund house at the end of every business day. A simplified formula to calculate NAV of a mutual fund is as follows:

NAV[55] = [{Market Value of Securities} – {Payables}] / {Number of units outstanding of the scheme}

Expense ratio (or Management expense ratio)

This is a metric which lets an investor know the total expenses of running a mutual fund as a percentage of an annual average value of its assets under management. The various kinds of expenses associated with a mutual fund are:

a. Management fee for investment professionals
b. Fees for audit, legal and other expenses
c. Transaction costs associated with asset transactions
d. Registrar fees for asset transfers
e. Custodian charges

Lower the expense ratio, higher are the returns to the investor. SEBI has capped the upper limit for expense ratios depending on the investment theme of the mutual fund scheme.

Type of fund	Permissible maximum expense ratio
Equity funds	2.5% of the average weekly net assets.
Debt funds	2.2.5% of the average weekly net assets
Index funds	1.5% of the average weekly net assets
Fund of funds	0.75% of the average weekly net assets

---

[55] The other aspects that are also considered in the complete formula are {Accrued Income}, {Receivables}, {Liabilities} and {Accrued expenses}

We observe that index funds and fund of funds have a lower permissible expense ratio limit. Can you think why? Index funds, for instance, are funds that invest the given money in the same proportion as the composition of the index it is mimicking. If it is a NIFTY index fund, then the money will be invested in the 30 index stock stocks of NIFTY in the same proportion that the NIFTY is comprised of. So it blindly follows the index. So no additional research overhead is present in these funds. This causes a drop in expenses and hence a lower expense ratio. Same is the case with fund of funds.

More information on Mutual funds and their performance

The interested reader can refer to the excellent resource on the internet www.valueresearchonline.com which is a neutral research agency that tracks the performance of all mutual funds in India for free. It also publishes a monthly magazine detailing mutual fund performances and investing recommendations. It also has data and fact sheets that are downloadable for free.

CHAPTER XIII

FUTURES and OPTIONS

Futures and Options, **F & O**, as they are commonly known as, are a class of financial instruments that derive their value from a host of different asset classes like stocks, bonds, currency, commodity and indices. These are constituents of a category of markets called **derivative markets**.

When you invest in Futures and Options, you are actually placing a bet on whether the value of the underlying asset it represents will increase or decrease by a certain percentage and within a set period of time. Hence, futures and options are different types of contracts or bets that get their value from existing or future prices of underlying securities.

FORWARD CONTRACT

Let us look at a hypothetical example to understand the concept of Forward Contracts. In a town, there lives a wholesale dealer, Mr.O, who sells Oranges. In the same

125

town is a large company called ***FreshOr*** that manufactures and sells bottled Orange juice. As Orange is seasonal fruit there is a great deal of fluctuation in its prices. Other factors that affect the prices of Oranges are global supply, local output, and climatic conditions.

1. Currently, *FreshOr* has an inventory of Oranges that is enough to produce juice for the next one month. To get a new supply *FreshOr* wants to source Oranges at a constant price as it thinks that the prices of Oranges can rise in the next month.

2. The wholesale dealer, Mr.O, wants to ensure that he sells Oranges at good prices and he thinks that for some reason, the prices of Oranges can fall in the next one month.

3. The procurement chief of *FreshOr* contacts Mr.O on **30-Sep-2014** and lays down the following proposal.

   a. Mr.O has to supply **100 metric ton**[56] of fresh Oranges on **31-Oct-2014** to FreshOr at a price of **Rs.44,500 per metric ton** which happens to be the market price of Oranges on **30-Sep-2014.**

   b. Oranges need to be of ***Common "blond" Oranges with Grade AA Organic*** variety.

   c. Mr.O needs to transport the **100 metric tons** of Oranges to *FreshOr*'s inventory warehouse.

---

[56] 1 metric ton = 1000 kilogram

    d. Mr.O agrees to the contract terms laid out by *FreshOr* and signs a contract. The contract looks like below[57].

    e. On the same day, 30-Sep-2014, Mr.O draws a contract promising to sell 100 metric tons of Oranges to FreshOr and FreshOr draws a contract promising to buy 100 metric tons of Oranges from Mr.O.

4. Both parties are bound by the contract and are obligated to fulfil the contract.

5. On **31-Oct-2014**, Mr.O delivers **100 metric tons** of Oranges of the said quality to *FreshOr*'s warehouse and receives a payment at the agreed price of **Rs.44,500 per metric ton**.

6. On **31-Oct-2014**, the market price of Oranges was **Rs.44,300 per metric ton**.

7. Mr.O stood to gain from this particular contract.

    a. Mr.O got **Rs.200 extra per metric ton** which is **Rs.20,000** extra that he made as he had this contract signed at **Rs.44,500**.

    b. *FreshOr* on the other hand lost **Rs.200** per metric ton as in the absence of the contract it could have sourced the Oranges from open market at **Rs.200 less per metric ton**. It lost **Rs.20,000** on this contract.

---

[57] Hypothetical contract note provided to clarify the concept of forward contracts

SAMPLE SELL (SHORT)
FORWARD CONTRACT

Contract Date: 30-Sep-2014

I (Mr.O) hereby promise to deliver **100 metric tons** of **Grade AA Organic "Blond" Common Oranges** on **31-Oct-2014** at a price of **Rs.44,500 per metric ton**. I promise to deliver 100 metric tons of Oranges to the warehouse of *FreshOr* at the following address - *FreshOr Warehouse*, Street 1A, Town Hall Road, Newtown.

Contract signed by both Mr.O and procurement chief of *FreshOr.*

SAMPLE BUY (LONG) FORWARD CONTRACT

Contract Date: 30-Sep-2014

FreshOr hereby agrees to buy **100 metric tons** of **Grade AA Organic "Blond" Common Oranges** on **31-Oct-2014** at a price of **Rs.44,500 per metric ton from Mr.O**. 100 metric tons of Oranges will be delivered by Mr.O to the warehouse of *FreshOr* at the following address - *FreshOr Warehouse*, Street 1A, Town Hall Road, Newtown.

Contract signed by both Mr.O and procurement chief of *FreshOr.*

This is called a **Forward Contract**. Forward contracts are **non-standardized contract** between two parties to buy or sell an asset at a specified future time at a price agreed upon today. Now, let's look at this contract and the transaction and try to understand how this works.

Need for Forward Contracts

As we can see, forward contracts provide both parties entering into the contract certain predictability to the price points.

1. For *FreshOr*, it helps because they are getting a new stock of Oranges for a price that is pre-defined and hence will not depend on whatever the market price of Oranges are on **31-Oct-2014**. It gets rid of the price uncertainty for *FreshOr*.

2. For *FreshOr*, their supply side of things is taken care of and they can concentrate on other aspects of the business.

3. It is a risk hedge for both Mr.O and *FreshOr* as it protects them from surprising price moves and provides some amount of stability to their respective businesses.

4. It gets a good view of demand for Mr.O who can plan well for his business given these definitive sales contracts. It brings in some amount of certainty to his business as well.

The two parties entering the contract normally have a contra view of the market but this may not always be the case. In this example, *FreshOr* believed that prices of

Oranges may rise in the next month while Mr.O believed that the prices of Oranges may fall in the next month. Actually, the prices of Oranges fell by about **Rs.200 per metric ton**.

Now, if the prices of Oranges had increased to **Rs.45,000** on **31-Oct-2014**, then FreshOr stood to have gained Rs.500 per metric ton or Rs.50,000 on the 100 metric tons because they would have got the 100 metric tons at the contractually agreed price of **Rs.44,500**. In this case, Mr.O would have lost Rs.50,000 as he had to abide by the contract at the agreed price of Rs.44,500.

SELL (Short) side

Mr.O is the SELLER of the forward contract whereby he promises to deliver oranges at a certain price, delivery date, quality and a certain specified price. He is said to be holding a **short** position. He is said to be short because he is trying to sell something that he does not possess when he is entering the contract.

BUY (Long) side

FreshOr is the BUYER of the forward contract whereby he promises to buy oranges at a certain price, delivery date, quality and a certain specified price. He is said to be the party that is going **long**. He is said to be holding a LONG position.

Forward Price

The price at which the forward contract is signed is called Strike Price. Here the forward price is Rs.44,500 per metric ton.

Counter-Party Risk

We have until now seen how **forward contracts** works. As discussed, it is a non-standardized agreement between two parties, one of which is interested to BUY an asset at a later date, price and quantity and another which is interested to SELL the asset. It is all well and good if both parties abide by the contract. But there is a potential risk associated with this contract that is described below:

Consider the example we discussed where Mr.O and *FreshOr* entered into a Forward Contract.

What happens if *FreshOr*, on the day of delivery, decides to reject the contract and instead buy Oranges from the open market because it is available for Rs.200 less than the market price? Mr.O will then suffer a huge amount of loss or has to pursue other legal options which may take its own time to reach a logical end.

Similar risk lies with FreshOr. What if, Mr.O, on the day of delivery, informs *FreshOr*, that he will not be able to provide 100 metric tons of Oranges at the said price? *FreshOr*, will then face a great deal of trouble because it has very little time to get a large supply of Oranges.

This risk that each party faces in a Forward Contract is called **Counter-Party Risk**.

FUTURES or FUTURE CONTRACTS

The presence of **counter-party risk** with forward contracts led to the idea of a standardized contract which is mediated by a futures exchange which absorbs the counter-party risk. The future exchange is regulated by the capital market regulator, that is, SEBI in India.

What are standardized future contracts?

Think of a standard contract template which will read as follows:

SAMPLE SELL (SHORT) FUTURE CONTRACT TEMPLATE

October 2014 FUTURES

I hereby promise to deliver **1 metric ton** of **Grade AA Organic "Blond" Common Oranges** on **31-Oct-2014** at a price of **Rs.44,500 per metric ton**.

SAMPLE BUY (LONG) FUTURE CONTRACT TEMPLATE

October 2014 FUTURES

I hereby promise to buy **1 metric ton** of **Grade AA Organic "Blond" Common Oranges** on **31-Oct-2014** at a price of **Rs.44,500 per metric ton**.

This is now a standard template to buy or sell 1 metric ton of Grade AA Organic "Blond" common oranges. *FreshOr*, can now go to the futures market and purchase 100 of these future contracts as it needs 100 metric tons of Oranges. The price at which it will buy the Oranges earlier was decided through a discussion between FreshOr and Mr.O. However, in this case, the futures exchange market decides on the prices of the Oranges for delivery in Oct 2014. The futures market will ensure that on the contract expiry date, *FreshOr* will have the 100 metric tons of Oranges delivered at their warehouse. The counter party risk is eliminated as it is no longer dependent on Mr.O fulfilling the contract but a host of others who have bought the SELL futures contracts who will be fulfilling the 100 metric ton order.

Margin

The inquisitive reader may ask as to how the counter party risk is eliminated by futures exchange market. It is a good question to ask!! Futures exchange requires both parties (the people going LONG and SHORT) to put up an initial amount of cash called **Margin**. The margin money is normally set as a percentage of the value of the futures contract. This money always needs to be maintained in the accounts of the people entering into the contract.

Open Interest (OI)

Any contract requires a buyer and a seller. One contract is formed when a buyer and seller agree on the transaction. Once a contract is formed, both buyer and seller are quite literally interested in the outcome of the contract. A pool of all such contracts where the outcome is yet to be determined is called Open Interest.

Open interest of futures is

1. The total number of options and /or futures that are not closed or delivered on a particular day
2. The total BUY market orders before the stock market open.

Open interest can also be defined as the total number of futures (futures contracts) or option contracts that have not yet been exercised, expired, or fulfilled by delivery. For each seller of Futures, they should be a buyer. Thus a seller and buyer combine to create 1 contract.

Open interest position is reported each day in the futures market for all products and it represents the increase or decrease in the number of contracts for that day, shown either as a positive or negative number as the case may be.

Open interest is an important indicator of trends and trend reversals for futures and option contracts.

Price Trend	Open Interest Trend	Interpretation
Increasing	**Increasing**	Strong market. Bullish sentiment
Increasing	**Declining**	Weakening market. Bearish signal. Declining OI means that the market is liquidating with people closing their positions and indicates prevailing price trend to go down.
Declining	**Increasing**	Signals weak market. This is because, with price decline, if we see lot of OI it means that lot of people are opening positions with PUT Option positions thus leading to bearish market signals.
Declining	**Declining**	This is signal that market is strengthening. This is because a price decline with declining OI means that people are not opening new positions and hence means an end of the downtrend.

Daily Settlement Process

Let's understand the daily settlement and margin money concepts with the help of an illustration. Let's say *FreshOr* goes LONG (on 30-Sep-2014) for 100 metric tons of Oranges in the futures exchange market for 14-Oct-2014 delivery, instead of going to Mr.O. Now, let's tabulate the margin money and settlement numbers on a daily basis.

Observe the calculations below. We will now see how this works.

1. On 30-Sep-2014, *FreshOr* purchases 100 metric tons LONG Orange futures for delivery on 14-Oct-2014. The price of futures on 30-Sep-2014 was **Rs.44,500 per metric ton**. The total contract value was Rs.44,500 * 100 = Rs.44,50,000 (Forty four lakhs and fifty thousand).

2. *FreshOr*, according to the rules of the futures exchange has to now pay the margin money. Let's say, margin money for Orange futures is **15% of the contract value** as set by the futures exchange. So, FreshOr, deposits 15% of the contract value as deposit money in its account with the exchange which amounts to 0.15 * Rs.44,50,000 = Rs.6,67,500.

ILLUSTRATION OF A TYPICAL FUTURE CONTRACT DAILY SETTLEMENT PROCESS						
Date	Metric tons	Price of Orange future	Contract Value	Margin Money	Final settlement	Daily Settlement Amount	Notes
30-Sep-14	100	44,500	4,450,000	667,500		-	FreshOr went LONG and paid margin money of 15% of the total contract value
1-Oct-14		44,621	4,462,100			12,100	Difference in Prices are settled on a daily basis and credited to FreshOr's bank account
2-Oct-14		44,758	4,475,800			13,700	
3-Oct-14		44,368	4,436,800			(39,000)	
4-Oct-14		44,291	4,429,100			(7,700)	
5-Oct-14		44,266	4,426,600			(2,500)	
6-Oct-14		44,456	4,445,600			19,000	
7-Oct-14		44,799	4,479,900			34,300	
8-Oct-14		44,104	4,410,400			(69,500)	
9-Oct-14		44,231	4,423,100			12,700	
10-Oct-14		44,564	4,456,400			33,300	
11-Oct-14		44,650	4,465,000			8,600	
12-Oct-14		44,575	4,457,500			(7,500)	
13-Oct-14		44,917	4,491,700			34,200	
14-Oct-14		45,048	4,504,800		3,782,500	13,100	FreshOr paid remaining money of 85% of the total contract value on contract expiry
Total						54,800	Total gains made by FreshOr due to the Futures Trade

3. On **1-Oct-2014**, the closing future price of Orange future was Rs.44,621 per metric ton. The closing prices are the last traded price of a future (at the close of day of the future exchange, normally at 11 PM).

4. As part of the daily settlement process, the difference amount (Rs.44621 – Rs.44500) * 100 metric tons = Rs.12,100 is credited to the bank account of *FreshOr* on 1-Oct-2014. This process is called daily settlement process.

5. On **2-Oct-2014**, the closing price of Orange future is Rs.44,758 per metric ton. Daily settlement process kicks after market close and deposits (Rs.44,758 – Rs.44,621) * 100 metric tons = Rs.13,700 in the bank account of *FreshOr*.

6. On **3-Oct-2014**, the day end closing prices of Orange futures drop significantly to Rs.44,368 per metric ton. As per daily settlement process, (Rs.44,368 – Rs.44,768) * 100 = -39000 is debited from *FreshOr*'s account.

7. This settlement process continues on a daily basis depending on the closing price of the future. On expiry, which is the technical term used for delivery of the contract, i.e. 14-Oct-2014, the closing price was Rs.45,048. The settlement process provides (Rs.45048 – Rs.44917) *100 = Rs.13,100 to *FreshOr*'s account. *FreshOr* also deposits the additional 85% of the contract money which is 85% of Rs.44,50,000 = Rs.37,82,500 in its account completing the delivery process.

8. In this entire transaction, *FutureOr* has made an additional gain of (Rs.45048 – Rs.44500) *100 = Rs.54800 which has got deposited in its bank account by a combination of daily credits and debits as part of settlement process.

This is the complete LONG side of the transactions. The SHORT (Sell) side of the transactions are a mirror image of these transactions except that they are in the opposite sign. For instance, the person who has gone SHORT on Orange futures after entering agreeing to sell at **Rs.44500**, will have lost (**Rs.44500 – Rs.45048) * 100 = - Rs.54,800**. That is, he agrees to sell at the lower price than a future market price. Even the SHORT seller will have to deposit the margin money upfront in the futures exchange account and he receives or loses money as part of the daily settlement process.

OPTIONS

Just like futures, Options are contracts between two parties which gives the buyer (the owner) the right, but not the obligation, to buy or sell and underlying asset or instrument at a specified strike price on or before a specified date. The seller has the corresponding obligation to fulfill the transaction (to sell or buy) – if the buyer (owner) exercises the option. The buyer pays a premium to the seller for its right.

Working of a CALL OPTION

Let's look at a very simple hypothetical example to understand the concept and the working of Option contracts. Two investors speculate about a particular stock Z which is trading at Rs.10 in the stock market.

1. The first investor, Mr.S1, thinks that the **stock will rise** in the next 30 days.

2. The second investor, Mr.S2, thinks that the **stock will drop** in the next 30 days.

Both S1 and S2 bet that their theory is right. So they decide to test who wins the bet.

Investor S1, says that he is ready to pay **Rs.1** per share as premium to S2 and reserves the right to buy 100 shares from him at **Rs.14.** Investor S2 agrees and accepts the bet. Investor S1, pays Rs.100 to S2.

Investor S1 is said to be the CALL OPTION BUYER. By paying the premium he has reserved his right to exercise his option to BUY 100 shares of Stock Z at **Rs.14** after 30 days.

Investor S2 is said to be the CALL OPTION SELLER (also called writer). He accepts the premium of Rs.1 per share from S1 and gets Rs.100 from S1. He has the obligation to SELL 100 shares of Stock Z at Rs.14 if S1 chooses to exercise the CALL OPTION.

Scenario 1: After 30 days, they meet again to check the results of the bet. They check the price of Stock Z and find that the market price of Z is **Rs.17.** Investor S1, immediately exercises his right to BUY 100 shares of Z at Rs.14 from S2. He then sells it immediately in the market at Rs.17. He makes a net profit of Rs.200 from the trade as he has paid Rs.1400 for 100 shares and 100 rupees as premium making the purchase price of stock Z as 15. The return on investment for S1 on this trade is 200% as he had invested only Rs.100 as premium to take a CALL position in stock Z.

Investor S2, on the on the other hand, could have sold the stock at 17 in the open market but was obligated to the CALL OPTION sell contract and had to sell the stock at 14. His net selling price was 15 as he had accepted Rs.100 as premium earlier. So his net loss from the trade is **Rs.200**.

In real-life though, investor **S1** can exercise the option on any day in the next **30 days** ideally whenever the market price is more than the strike price + premium total. CALL OPTION is now said to be **in the money.**

Scenario 2: After 30 days, they meet again to check the results of the bet. They check the price of Stock Z and find that the market price of Z is **Rs.12**. Investor S1, does not exercise his right to BUY 100 shares of Z at Rs.14 from S2. His purchase price has been **Rs.15** on the CALL OPTION. So, he will rather purchase the shares in the open market than pay Rs.14 by exercising his option. CALL OPTION is now said to be **out of money.** Net loss booked by S1 is **Rs.100**. Loss % is 100%.

Investor S2, on the other hand, makes a net profit of Rs.100. He still continues to hold the 100 shares of Stock Z as investor S1 has not chosen to exercise his CALL BUY option.

Scenario 3: If the market price of the stock Z is Rs.14 after 30 days, the CALL OPTION is said to be at the money. It is best not to exercise the option and book a loss of Rs.100 (paid as premium) even in this case. Loss % is 100%.

Working of a PUT OPTION

Let's look at a very simple hypothetical example. Two investors speculate about a particular stock Y which is trading at **Rs.10** in the stock market.

1. The first investor, Mr.S1, thinks that the **stock will drop** in the next 30 days.
2. The second investor, Mr.S2, thinks that the **stock will rise** in the next 30 days.

Both S1 and S2 bet that their theory is right. So they decide to test who wins the bet.

Investor S1, says that he is ready to pay **Rs.1** per share as premium to S2 and reserves the right to SELL **100 shares** to him at **Rs.7.** Investor S2 agrees and accepts the bet. Investor S1, pays Rs.100 to S2.

Investor S1 is said to be the PUT OPTION BUYER. By paying the premium he has reserved his right to exercise his option to SELL 100 shares of Stock Y to S2 at **Rs.7** after 30 days.

Investor S2 is said to be the PUT OPTION SELLER. He accepts the premium of **Rs.1 per share** from S1 and gets **Rs.100** from S1. He has the obligation to BUY 100 shares of Stock Y at Rs.7 if S1 chooses to exercise the PUT OPTION.

Scenario 1: After 30 days, they meet again to check the results of the bet. They check the price of Stock Y and find that the market price of Y is **Rs.4**. Investor S1, immediately exercises his right to SELL 100 shares of Y at Rs.7 to S2. He purchases 100 shares of Y from the market at Rs.4 and sells it at Rs.7 to S2. He makes a net profit of **Rs.200** from the trade (as he has paid a premium of Rs100 for the PUT OPTION). The return on investment for S1 on this trade is 200% as he had invested only Rs.100 as premium to take a PUT position in stock Y.

Investor S2, on the on the other hand, could have bought the stock at Rs.4 in the open market but was obligated to the PUT OPTION BUY contract and had to BUY the stock at Rs.7. His net buying price was 6 as he had accepted Rs.100 as premium earlier. So his net loss from the trade is **Rs.200**.

In real-life though, investor **S1** can exercise the option on any day in the next **30 days** ideally whenever the market price is less than the strike price + premium total. PUT OPTION is now said to be **in the money.**

Scenario 2: After 30 days, they meet again to check the results of the bet. They check the price of Stock Y and find that the market price of Y is **Rs.12**. Investor S1, does not exercise his right to SELL 100 shares of Y at **Rs.7** to S2 as he will have to first purchase the stock Y at Rs.12 from the market and sell it to S2 for Rs.7 which is a loss. PUT

OPTION is now said to be **out of money.** Net loss booked by S1 is **Rs.100**. Loss % is 100%.

Investor S2, on the other hand, makes a net profit of **Rs.100** from premium he received from S1.

Scenario 3: If the market price of the stock Y is Rs.7 after 30 days, the PUT OPTION is said to be at the money. It is best not to exercise the option and book a loss of Rs.100 (paid as premium) even in this case. Loss % is 100%.

OPTION contract

The previous illustrations were hypothetical. In real life, the options trading happen through the futures and options market regulated by SEBI. The following example is closer to real life.

Consider an investor Mr.I who has studied the fundamental and technical aspects of the publicly traded company called *Fair Builders*[58]. He is bullish about this company and thinks that the share price of this company will rise in the next 3 months (SEP-2014) from its current market price of **Rs.20** (JUL-2014). What are various things he can do in such a scenario?

1. **Stock Market investment to BUY shares:** A straightforward thing to do is to purchase stocks of *Fair Builders* and then sell it after the necessary price targets has been reached. This is what was discussed in the chapter on Stock

[58] Fictitious company

Markets. If he purchases **10,000** shares of *Fair Builders* for **Rs.20,** the total investment required for the transaction is 10000 * 20 = Rs.2,00,000 + transaction charges + brokerage charges.

2. **BUY CALL OPTIONS:** Another thing Mr.I can do is to buy a CALL option in the F & O market at a **premium of Rs.2 per share** for **strike price of Rs.30** which will give him the right to BUY shares of *Fair Builders* between the day it was purchased till the CALL option expiry date. Say he purchases 10,000 CALL options by paying Rs.2 per share as premium. The total amount of money he invests in this transaction is 10,000 * 2 =Rs.20,000.

Let's now try and understand the CALL OPTIONS a little better. Just like futures contract, we have two people entering into a contract through a futures exchange. The exchange absorbs the counter-party risk as usual. The difference in this contract and the futures contract is that the base asset class of the options is stocks, currency, index and so on but not commodities. The CALL OPTIONS are normally cash settled and there is no delivery of an asset at the expiry. Moreover, the two parties entering the futures contracts are obligated to adhere to the contract whereas in OPTIONS, the buyer of the OPTION has the right but not an obligation to exercise the OPTION.

Say, Mr.I, purchased 10,000 CALL OPTIONS of the stock at a strike price of Rs.30 by paying Rs.2 per share as premium. The total contract value is Rs.2,00,000 (i.e.10,000 shares * Rs.20 per share) which is the position he has taken with an investment of just **Rs.20,000**. This is called leverage.

Scenario 1: Out of Money: Now, say in Sep-2014, when the OPTIONS contract expires, the price of the stock *Fair Builders* is Rs.25. Mr.I's CALL OPTION is worthless because he has to pay Rs.30 to buy the OPTION whereas the market price is Rs.25. So he can book a loss of Rs.20,000 and not choose to exercise the buy option. This is called OPTION being **Out of Money.** The option is **out of money** till it reaches the price Rs.32 (Rs.30 strike price + Rs.2 premium). His loss is 100% in this case.

Scenario 2: In the Money: Now, say in Sep-2014, on the day OPTIONS contract expires, the price of the stock *Fair Builders* is Rs.38. Mr.I's CALL OPTION is now said to be **in the money.** This is because he can now exercise the CALL OPTION to buy 10,000 shares of *Fair Builders* at **Rs.30** as per the contract and sell it immediately in the open market at Rs.38. This will give him a profit of (38-30-2) = Rs.6 per share and the profit is Rs.60,000. The Return on investment is 300% because he had invested only Rs.20,000 to start with to BUY the CALL OPTION.

Scenario 3: At the Money: If the price of *Fair Builders* is Rs.30 in Sep-2014 on the day of Option expiry, the OPTION is said to be **at the money**. Even in this case, there is a net loss in exercising the BUY option and hence it will be a loss making proposition.

Call option – profit and loss diagram

The preceding discussion on CALL and PUT options can be diagrammatically represented using profit and loss diagrams.

Scenario –

1000 CALL options for Stock A for strike price of Rs.50 bought at a premium of Rs.4 per option.

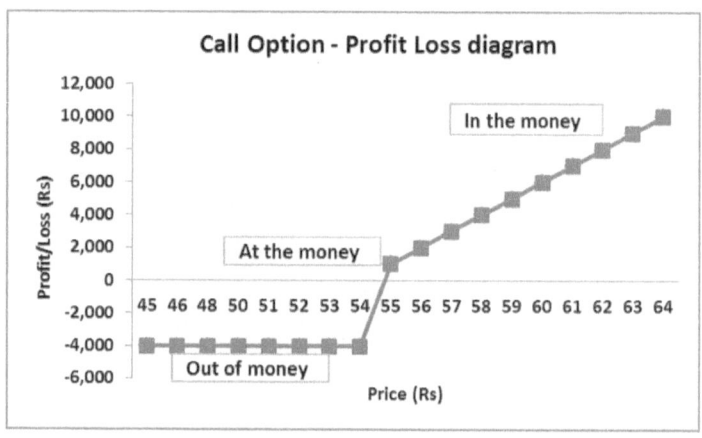

Explanation – This is a typical profit loss diagram for a **long call**. (Call option)

1. The x-axis in the graph is the price and the y-axis is the profit/loss at each of these prices. For all the prices below strike price (Rs.50) we observe that the option is at net loss of Rs.4,000 (**Out of Money**).

2. In the price range 50 to 54, the call option is **at the money**. However, it is still not profitable because Rs.4 as premium was paid.

3. Only above **Rs.54**, does the option move into the positive territory and starts to give profits for every upward move. This range above 54, is when the option is **in the money**.

Put option – profit and loss diagram

Scenario – Consider a trader who has bought the Put option.

1000 PUT options for Stock A for strike price of Rs.50 bought at a premium of Rs.4 per option.

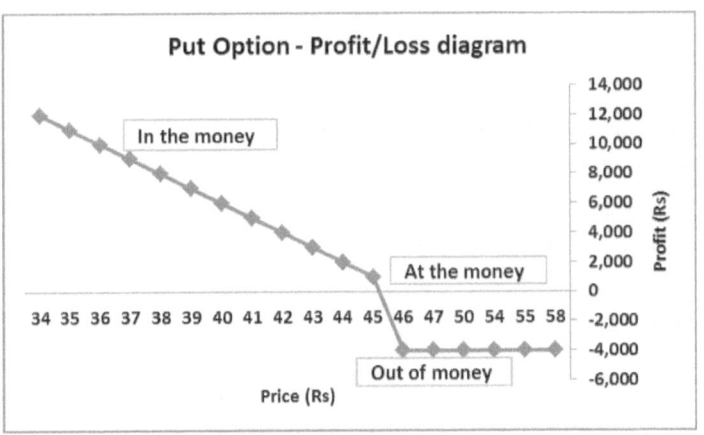

Explanation – This is a typical profit loss diagram for a **long put**. (Put option)

1. The x-axis in the graph is the price and the y-axis is the profit/loss at each of these prices. For all

the prices above strike price (Rs.50) we observe that the option is at net loss of **Rs.4,000 (Out of Money)**.

2. In the price range 50 to 46, the call option is **at the money**. However, it is still not profitable because Rs.4 was paid as premium.

3. Only below **Rs.46**, does the put option move into the positive territory and starts to give profits for every downward move. This range below 46, is when the option is **in the money.**

Strike Price

Strike or exercise price is the price at which the underlying security can be bought or sold as specified in the OPTION Contract. In the above example the strike price is **Rs.30**. The investor Mr.I is convinced that the stock will appreciate by at least more than **Rs.10** from its current market price of **Rs.20**. Hence he bets on strike price of Rs.30 by paying a premium of **Rs.2 per share** making his effective price of acquisition of Rs.32 to breakeven in the investment.

Expiry

The expiration date of the option contract is the date after which the option contract is no longer valid.

American and European Style Options

There are two styles of OPTION contracts.

1. **American style option** – the right to exercise this option exists between the start and expiry date of the contract.
2. **European style option** – the right to exercise this option exists only on the date of expiry of the contract. So the BUYER of the option (CALL or PUT) has to hold on to the option once he has bought it until the contract expiry.

Indian capital markets follow American style options.

Types of Options and Participants

There are two types of OPTION contracts. CALL option and PUT option.

CALL OPTION – As seen earlier, CALL OPTION gives the buyer of the OPTION the right but not the obligation to buy the underlying instrument. Every call option has two participants, **CALL BUYER** and **CALL SELLER**.

In general,

1. **CALL BUYER** is an investor who has a bullish outlook about the underlying asset and in the timeframe considered.
2. **CALL SELLER** is an investor who has a bearish outlook about the underlying asset and the timeframe considered.

Premium of CALL OPTIONS are higher for lower strike prices. We will try and understand this with an example. A stock trading at Rs.10 is highly likely to make it to Rs.12 rather than Rs.20 in 30 days. So, the premium (option price) for strike price of 12 will be higher than the premium charged for strike price of Rs.20.

PUT OPTION – The buyer of this OPTION has the right but not the obligation to SELL the underlying instrument. Every PUT option has two participants, **PUT BUYER** and **PUT SELLER**.

In general,

1. **PUT BUYER** is an investor who has a bearish outlook about the underlying asset[59] in the timeframe considered.
2. **PUT SELLER** is an investor who has a bullish outlook about the underlying asset in the timeframe considered.

Premium of PUT OPTIONS are higher at higher strike prices. This is again intuitive because the propensity of a stock reaching Rs.20 from Rs.22 is more likely in a given time period than the propensity of it reaching Rs.10. Hence **PUT OPTION** with a strike price of Rs.20 will have a higher premium than the **PUT OPTION** at a strike price of Rs.10.

Put to Call Ratio

PUT to CALL ratio is a well-known contrarian sentiment indicator that shows PUT volume relative to CALL

---

[59] Hence he is selling the asset

volume. PUT options are used as a hedge against market weakness or bet on a decline. CALL options are used as a hedge against market strength or bet on advance.

PUT/CALL Ratio = {PUT Volume/CALL Volume}

Clearly, PUT /CALL ratio will be greater than 1 when PUT volumes are greater than CALL volumes and are below 1 when PUT volumes are lesser than CALL volumes.

This indicator is used to gauge market sentiment.

1. **PUT/CALL** at high levels (much greater than 1) is deemed to signal bearish outlook as PUT option volumes indicate bearish outlook.
2. **PUT/CALL** at low levels (much less than 1) is deemed to signal a bullish outlook as CALL option volumes indicates bullish outlook.

Contrarian sentiment works just the opposite to what was described about. Contrarians argue that:

1. If PUT/CALL is at historic high levels (much greater than 1) then it can be viewed as a BULLISH signal because most of the market is speculating a bearish and this over-pessimism is an opportunity to find value picks (as things cannot get worse) leading to revival.
2. If PUT/CALL is at historic low levels, it can be viewed as a BEARISH signal because there is excessive optimism in investors leading to prices being pushed to the brim and the market is very

speculative. It is viewed as a time when the bubble will burst and trends will go downwards.

Index Options

Index Options are derivative instruments whose underlying assets are the various indices discussed earlier. Let's consider an example.

Scenario – Index CALL Option

1. Ace investor, Mr.I thinks that NIFTY index will safely cross **8300** by Jan 2015.
2. He has come to this conclusion by studying various parameters of the market such as macro-economic scenario, index stock performances, broad market sentiment, weather predictions, and government policies.
3. He decides to place a bet in the market that **NIFTY** index will safely cross **8300** by **Jan 2015**.
4. He goes ahead and buys a CALL index option. NSE website[60] details the premium associated with all the current option contracts in the NSE options market.

---

[60] Reader can refer to the NSE website which lists the current equity derivative prices: http://www.nseindia.com/live_market/dynaContent/live_watch/derivative_stock_watch.htm

Instrument Type	Symbol	Expiry Date	Option Type	Strike Price
Index Options	NIFTY	29-Jan-15	CALL	8300.00

151.00	Prev Close	Open	High	Low	Close
	148.90	141.00	155.00	126.60	148.90

5. Mr.I bought an Index CALL Option with a **strike price of 8300** in NIFTY. The option expires on **29-Jan-2015**. The premium (option price) for this bet is available at **Rs.151**. Mr.I buys 1 lot (**25** options) by paying a premium of **Rs.151 per option**.

6. Minimum lot quantity that requires to be bought currently is set at 25.

7. The total contract value is **25 * 8300 = Rs.2,07,500**

8. Mr.I pays the price of option at **Rs.151** per option and pays **25 * 151 = Rs.3,775.**

9. To reiterate, CALL options give Mr.I the right to BUY the underlying asset at the strike price.

10. The option is **in the money** only if it reaches a value greater than 8300 + 151 = 8451 on or before 29-Jan-2015.

11. Suppose on **15-Jan-2015**, the index reaches 8490, Mr.I can immediately execute the option at a given option price and earn a profit of (8490 − 8300 − 151) * 25 = **Rs.975.** The return on investment is 975/3775 = **26%** on an investment of **Rs.3,775.**

12. Suppose, in the entire month, the index does not reach 8300 and ends at **8290** on 29-Jan-2015 then the 1 lot of options (**25 CALL** options) that Mr.I has is worthless (value equal to 0). He loses

Rs.3,775, the premium paid for the option. The option is said to be **out of money**.

Scenario – Index PUT Option

1. Ace investor, Mr.I thinks about covering his risk of being **out of money** in the CALL Option. He is trying to grapple with the question – what if NIFTY index will not cross **8250** by Jan 2015?
2. So he decides to cover his losses by going for a PUT Index Option on NIFTY.
3. He decides to place a PUT Index Option bet in the market that **NIFTY** index will not cross **8250** by **Jan 2015**.
4. He goes ahead and buys a PUT index option. NSE website details the premium associated with all the current option contracts in the NSE options market.
5. A PUT index option is a SELL option at the strike price of **8250**.

Instrument Type	Symbol	Expiry Date	Option Type	Strike Price
Index Options	NIFTY	29-Jan-15	PUT	8250.00

89.45	Prev Close	Open	High	Low	Close
	96.30	106.85	113.00	85.00	90.80

6. Mr.I bought an Index PUT Option with a **strike price of 8250** in NIFTY. The option expires on **29-Jan-2015**. The premium (option price) for this bet is available at **Rs.89.45**. Mr.I buys 1 lot (**25**

options) by paying a premium of **Rs.89.45 per option**.

7. Minimum lot quantity that requires to be bought currently is set at 25.

8. The total contract value is **25 * 8250 = Rs.2,06,250**

9. Mr.I pays the price of option at **Rs.89.45** per option and pays **25 * 89.45 = Rs.2,236.**

10. The option is **in the money** only if it reaches a value less than strike price of 8250 – 89.45 = **8160** on or before 29-Jan-2015.

11. Suppose on **15-Jan-2015**, the index reaches 8100, Mr.I can immediately execute the option at a given option price and earn a profit of **(8160 – 8100) * 25 = Rs.1500**.

12. Suppose, in the entire month, the index does not reach 8250 and ends at **8340** on 29-Jan-2015 then the 1 lot of options (**25 PUT** options) that Mr.I has is worthless (value equal to 0). He loses **Rs.2,236**, the premium paid for the option. The option is said to be **out of money**.

Let's now compare the pricing of **CALL** and **PUT** options together and see the profitability in various scenarios.

SCENARIO	CALL OPTION (25 – 1 lot) {Breakeven at 8451} Premium Paid = Rs.3775	PUT OPTION (25 – 1 lot) {Breakeven at 8160} Premium Paid: Rs.2236	PROFIT/ (LOSS) {Total premium: 6011}
NIFTY closes at **8340** on 29-Jan-2015	Out of Money – Loss of premium	Out of Money – Loss of premium	**Total Loss = Rs.6,011**

NIFTY closes at **8560** on 29-Jan-2015	**In the Money – Exercise the right to BUY**	Worthless – Loss of premium	Total Profit[61] due to CALL option = Rs.2,725 Total Loss due to PUT option = Rs.2,236 **Net Profit = Rs.489**
NIFTY closes at **8160** on 29-Jan-2015	Out of Money – Loss of premium	At the money – Breakeven but worthless with loss of premium	**Total Loss = Rs.6,011**
NIFTY closes at **7980** on 29-Jan-2015	Out of Money – Loss of premium	**In the Money–Exercise the right to SELL**	Total Loss due to CALL option = Rs. 3,775 Total Profit due to PUT Option = Rs.4,500 **Net Profit = Rs.725**

Hedging

In the hypothetical scenario above, we have Mr.I investing in both CALL and PUT options. Can you think why? This is a risk mitigation mechanism. Note that the CALL option will start making money for the investor when the index moves up whereas the PUT option will start making money when the index moves down. So, theoretically, it is making sure our investment is protected regardless of

---

[61] $(8560 - 8300 - 151) * 25 = $ Rs.2,725

how the market moves. Note that this does not eliminate the risk altogether but reduces it to a certain extent. This concept of limiting the risk is called **Hedging**.

Hedging is akin taking out an insurance policy. Once you buy a car (asset – analogous to the investment), you buy a vehicle insurance to protect your car against some known issues like accident, wear and tear, theft, other damage and so on. The insurance comes at a cost, and that is the investment you are making to protect your asset. The question that one has to ask is when do I take a hedge? I buy a new pen worth Rs.400. Do I then get an insurance protection cover for my pen? No!! We won't unless the new pen we bought is worth a few lakh rupees!! Hedging is generally done for a large portfolio of assets where losses can be astronomical if they are not risk-insulated.

Hedging – An illustrative example

Mr.G, who now owns a large fund, has a large asset under maintenance (AUM) which he needs to take care of. He always uses hedging to ensure that the portfolio risk is minimized[62]. Let's examine how he does this.

---

[62] This particular strategy is called **married put** strategy. There are many such hedging strategies to minimize risk.

Txn #	Transaction	Bought On	Contract Expiry	Number of shares/ Options	Price / Option Premium	Strike Price	Total Investment	Investor Outlook
A	Purchase of Stock A	1-Sep-14	NA	20,000	50	NA	10,00,000	Optimistic
B	Purchase of PUT Option of Stock A (European Style option)	1-Sep-14	30-Nov-14	40,000	4	40	1,60,000	Pessimistic
Total							**11,60,000**	

1. **Transaction A:** Mr.G is a big fan of a company A, whose stock has been doing an excellent run in the stock market. Currently, stock of A, is trading at Rs.50. Mr.G thinks that stock of company A is bound to increase in the next 3 months. Being an optimistic investor, he invests Rs.10 lacs in stock A. He has thus bought 20,000 shares of stock A at Rs.50 apiece. Mr.G has an optimistic outlook for the next 3 months for stock A.

2. **Transaction B:** The pessimist in Mr.G warns him that there is a downside risk in investing so much money in just stock A and he needs to cover for his downside risk as far as possible. What will you do if the price of the stock crashed to half its value today? This question makes him think of a risk minimization plan to ensure he does not lose all his money should the price move in a downward spiral. Mr.G, comes up with a plan and purchases 40,000 PUT option contracts of the stock A by paying Rs.4 as premium for a strike price of 40 in the options market. All he is saying is, "should the market move downward below Rs.40, I will

exercise my right to PUT option thus profiting from the downside movement of the stock A thus minimizing the downside risk".

In other words *"As stock prices of company A moves up, Transaction A will be profitable and as market prices of stock A moves downwards, Transaction B will be profitable"*. So, have we uncorked a brilliant method to "always win" in the stock market? Not really! If this was the case, then markets won't have been as interesting as it is today. Risk mitigation can be done only to a certain extent. In the above example for instance, if the stock price of company A, ends up between 36 and 50, you are virtually in the loss zone because the stock you bought is not profitable or loss making and the PUT option is also out of the money. It is only when the stock prices move below Rs.36 that the PUT option becomes profitable but the stock is in a loss. Reverse is the case when the stock prices move up. Let's quickly look at a few scenarios that will help cement the understanding of the hedging concept.

Assumptions: To simplify the scenario, let's make some assumptions. The following assumptions may not hold in real life scenarios. This is purely being done to help convey the hedging concept clearly.

1. Options we've purchased are European style and hence it can be exercised only on the expiry date of the option.

2. Mr.G requires to sell the stock on the expiry date to pay back some of the redemptions (honor redemptions) on that day.

3. Let us ignore transaction and brokerage costs as they will not materially impact the results.

Scenario 1

Stock A loses steam and ends at **Rs.25 on 30-Nov-14**. Following transactions were done by Mr.G on 30-Nov-14.

Transaction	No. of shares/ options	Price	Strike Price	Total Profit / (Loss)
Sold stock A at Rs.25 booking a loss of Rs.5 lacs	20,000	25	NA	(5,00,000)
Exercise PUT option as it is in the money (buy the stock at market price of Rs.25 and sell at contract strike price of Rs.40). Adjust the initial premium paid of Rs.4 / option (40-25) * 40000 – 1,60,000 = Rs.4,40,000	40,000	25	40	4,40,000
TOTAL Profit/(Loss)				**Rs.(60,000)**

Unfortunately, Mr.G, makes a loss of Rs.60,000 as the stock A fell to Rs.25 from the invested price of Rs.50. But here's a bright spot. If Mr.G had only invested in 20,000 shares of A and it had fallen to Rs.25 his overall investment of Rs.10 lacs would have halved to Rs.5 lacs. A great loss indeed! But his risk mitigation plan of investing in PUT options came to his rescue. As the market went down, the price of stock A collapsed to reach Rs.25 at the end of 3 months. This made the PUT options to be **in the money** (profitable) and hence he exercised his PUT option. His profit due to options was Rs.4.4 lacs. Hence, of the Rs.5 lacs that he lost in stocks, he recovered Rs.4.4 lacs of that due to this risk mitigation effort. This is called the hedge. Though part of his portfolio was in a loss, he was able to ensure that the total loss is minimized to the extent possible.

Scenario 2

Stock A shoots up as expected by Mr.G and ends at **Rs.68 on 30-Nov-14**. Following transactions were done by Mr.G on 30-Nov-14.

Transaction	No. of shares/ options	Price	Strike Price	Total Profit / (Loss)
Sold stock A at Rs.68 booking a profit of Rs.3.6 lacs	20,000	68	NA	3,60,000
PUT option is **out of money**. The initial invested premium Rs.1,60,000 is booked as a loss. Option not exercized	40,000	4	40	(1,60,000)
TOTAL Profit/(Loss)				**Rs.2,00,000**

Mr.G's optimistic theory that stock A will increase has come true and he realized a profit of Rs.3,60,000 because of the sale of stock A. However, his hedge is now worthless and the investment that he made on buying the hedge Rs.1,60,000 is booked as a loss. The PUT option is not exercised as it is out of money. Total profit in this scenario is **Rs.2,00,000.**

Scenario 3

Share price of company A remains flat and ends at **Rs.47 on 30-Nov-14**. Following transactions were done by Mr.G on 30-Nov-14.

Transaction	No. of shares/ options	Price	Strike Price	Total Profit / (Loss)
Sold stock A at Rs.47 booking a loss of Rs.60,000	20,000	47	NA	(60,000)
PUT option is **out of money**. The initial invested premium Rs.1,60,000 is booked as a loss. Option not exercized	40,000	4	40	(1,60,000)
TOTAL Profit/(Loss)				**Rs.(2,20,000)**

In life, not everything is rosy. Not all trades make profits. In this scenario, Mr.G, realizes that even though he tried his best to hedge the investments he was making, he risks losses. Stock A, did not increase but decreased by Rs.3 and ended at Rs.47 after three months. Mr.G sold his shares at a loss of Rs.3 per share booking a loss of Rs.60,000 because of shares. Unfortunately, the PUT option is out of money as well because the strike price is 40 whereas the stock ended up at 47. So, he booked losses to the extent of premium paid i.e. Rs.1,60,000. His total portfolio loss because of investment in Stock A was Rs.2,20,000.

These 3 scenarios paint an overall picture of hedging and its effects on the performance of a portfolio. This concept also explains one of the known phenomena in capital markets. The Put-to-Call ratio we discussed earlier, almost always tends to be greater than 1 because of the heavy hedge PUT options done by institutional investors to minimize downside risks to their large portfolios.

Compendium of commonly used capital market terminology

Abbreviation	Description
200DMA	200 Day Moving Average of share prices. The trend provides a good view of the price trend.
ADR	American Depository Receipts
BCD	Bond Currency Derivatives
BSE	Bombay Stock Exchange
CAD	Current A/c Deficit
CAGR	Compounded Annual Growth Rate
CALL	RIGHT but not the obligation to BUY in derivatives market
CAPM	Capital Asset Pricing Model (mathematical model used in Option pricing)
CBOVI	Chicago Board Options Volatility Index
CFS	Cash Future Spread
CMP	Current Market Price
CRAR	Capital to Risk Asset Ratio
CRR	Cash Reserve Ratio

Abbreviation	Description
CTS	Cheque Truncation System
DEM	Debt to Equity Ratio
DGFT	Director General of Foreign Trade
DII	Direct Institutional Investor
DMA	Direct Market Access
DP	Depository Participant
EBIT	Earnings Before Interest and Tax
EBITDA	Earnings Before Interest, Tax, Depreciation and Amortization
ECB	External Commercial Borrowing / European Central Bank
ECR	Export Credit Re-finance
ECS	Electronic Clearance Service
EFP	Exchange of Futures for physical delivery
EPS	Earnings per Share (= Surplus profit/No. of equity shares)
ETF	Exchange Traded Fund
F&O	Futures and Options
FDI	Foreign Direct Investment
FEMA	Foreign Exchange Management Act
FII	Foreign Institutional Investors
FMC	Forward Contract Commission
FMCG	Fast Moving Consumer Goods
FPIR	Foreign Portfolio Investors Regulation
FPO	Follow On Public Offer
FRRB	Financial Reporting Review Board
GAAP	Generally Accepted Accounting Principals
GAAR	General Anti Avoidance Rules
HFT	High Frequency Trading
HNI	High Net-worth Individual

Abbreviation	Description
IBMA	Indian Bullion Market Association
IMPS	Immediate Payment Service – A real time money transfer service provided by almost all leading banks through national payment corporation of India and is available 24/7.
IPO	Initial Public Offer
KYC	Know Your Customer – A process of documenting the customer identity and keeping the records updated on an annual basis
LAF	Liquidity Adjustment Facility
LBRM	Lead Bank Running Manager
MCX	Multi Commodity Exchange
M0, M1	**Quantum of Money Supply**: Sum total of value of all coins and currency notes in circulation in a country and other money equivalents that are easily convertible to money. It is called narrow money.
M2	**Quantum of Money Supply**: M0 + M1 + Short Term Deposits with the banks + 24 hour money market funds
M3	**Quantum of Money Supply**: M2 + Long Term Deposits with the banks + Money market funds more than 24 hours
M4	**Quantum of Money Supply**: M3 + Other Deposits **(M2, M3 or M4 are also termed as Broad Money)**
MF	Mutual Fund
MFI	Micro Finance Institution
MSF	Marginal Standing Facility
MTM (M2M)	Marked to Market
MUDRA	Micro Units Development Refinance Agency – This provides credit (loans) at reasonable cost to small business units (program launched in 2015)

Abbreviation	Description
NAV	Net Asset Value of a Mutual Fund
NBFC	Non-banking Financial Corporation
NCDEX	National Commodity and Derivative Exchange
NCFM	National Certification in Financial Markets – Entry level examination modules to be cleared to be an equity market dealer
NEAT	National Exchange for automated trading
NFO	New Fund Offer
NIFTY	NSE key market index comprising of 50 stocks called **NIFTY50**
NISM	National Institute of Securities Markets
NPA	Non-Performing Assets
NSCCL	National Securities Clearing Corporation Ltd. is the institution responsible for the post sale processes after a stock transaction. It settles the trades executed on exchanges working with clearing members, custodians, clearing banks and depositories.
NSE	National Stock Exchange
NSEL	National Spot Exchange is designated agency for commodity trading
ODI	Offshore Derivative Instrument (P-Note)
OFS	Offer for sale
OI	Open Interest
OMO	Open Market Operation
OPINC	Operating Income
OTC	Over The Counter trade
PAN	Permanent Account Number
PB ratio	Price to Book ratio
PE firm	Private Equity Firm
PE ratio	Price to Equity ratio
PLR	Prime Lending Rate

Abbreviation	Description
PMI	Purchasing Manager's Index
PUT	RIGHT but not an obligation to SELL in derivatives market
P-Note	Participatory Note
QARC	Qualified Audit Review Committee
QIB	Qualified Institutional Buyer
QoQ	Quarter on Quarter
QTD	Quarter To Date
REER	Real Effective Exchange Rate (trade weighted exchange rate adjusted for inflation rate differentials.)
Repo Rate	Interest rate at which the central bank (RBI) lends money to commercial banks in the event of shortfall of funds. It is an inflation controlling lever available with the central bank. An increase in repo rate will force the commercial banks to borrow less and hence the money supply in the system will decrease leading to controlling inflation
Reverse Repo	Interest rate at which the central bank (RBI) borrows money from commercial banks in the event of shortfall of funds. An increase in reverse repo will mean that the commercial banks will park funds with central bank thus decreasing the money supply in the system
ROCE	Return on Capital Employed
ROE	Return on Equity
ROI	Return on Investment
SAAR	Specific Anti-Avoidance Rules
SEBI	Securities and Exchange Board of India
SENSEX	Key stock market index of BSE comprising of 30 stocks
SLR	Statutory Liquidity Ratio
SUUTI	Specified Undertaking Unit Trust of India

Abbreviation	Description
T + 2	**T + 2** settlement cycle indicates the Transaction Date + 2 days of time on which the transactions will be closed
TIN	Tax Information Network
TOR	Turn Over Ratio
TTM	Trailing Twelve Months (timeframe of last 12 months used in financial reporting)
VC	Venture Capitalist
VSAT	Very Small Aperture Terminal
YoY	Year on Year
YTD	Year To Date

A brief note on some additional concepts of Capital Market

Terminology	Description
AGM	Annual general body meeting, held every year, has the purpose of electing the company board of directors and pass any important resolutions like dividend declaration, bonus declaration and inform the shareholders the strategic direction the company is pursuing.
Arbitrage	Arbitrage is simultaneous purchase and sale of a security (or an asset) in order to profit from a difference in the price. It is a trade that profits by exploiting price differences of identical or similar financial instruments, on different markets or in different forms.
Algorithmic Trading	It is a trading method which is program driven.

Terminology	Description
ASBA	Applications Supported by Blocked Amount. It is a process developed by SEBI to block the amount of the investor during an IPO application process. The IPO investor's bank account is not debited until shares are allotted to him/her. This in turn saves lot of effort by eliminating the need for refund check processing transactions.
BASEL III Norms	It is a comprehensive set of reforms measures which focuses primarily on the level of loss reserves that banks are required to hold. BASELIII focuses primarily on the risk run by the bank by requiring different levels of reserves for different forms of bank deposits and other borrowings.
BEARS (Bear Market)	A sharp prolonged decline in the price of assets (stocks) in the equity markets is a defined feature of BEAR market. Generally it is believed that when equity market fall over 20% (percent) from their peaks they are in the BEAR territory.
BULLS (Bull Market)	A sharp prolonged increase in the price of assets (stocks) in the equity markets is a defined feature of BULL market. Generally it is believed that when equity market increase over 20% (percent) from their peaks they are in the BULL territory.
Blue Chip Stocks	Name given to the shares that are considered as safe investment.
Brown Field	Investing in existing business
Capital Infusion	It is done with the twin objectives of adequately meeting the credit requirements of the protective sectors of economy as well as to maintain regular capital adequacy ratio.
Circuit Limit	A circuit limit ensures that the price of a script cannot move upward or downward beyond a limit set for the day (usually it is +-20%, +-10%, +-5% of the previous day closing price of the stock).
Credit Rating Agency	As per SEBI regulation every debt security like bonds or debentures should be rated by credit rating agencies like CRISIL, ICRA CARE.

Terminology	Description
Current Account Deficit	Current A/c deficit arises when a country's total imports of goods services and transfers exceed export. Latest data shows that CAD of India is about 6.7%.
Cut-off Price	It is the price at which the shares will be allotted usually the cut-off price is the weighted average price of the various bids in a book-building IPO. It is also called floor price, the minimum price at which shares can be sold through IPO or EPO.
Delivery	Stocks bought to hold for a period of time are said to be taken as delivery. They will be credited to ones Demat account after T + 2 trade settlement cycle.
Direct Market Access	This allows brokers to offer clients direct access to exchange through their infrastructure without their manual intervention. It minimizes the risk of manual order entry.
EPFO	Employee Provident Fund Organization
Employee Stock Options	A stock option gives an employee of the company the right to buy a certain number of shares in the company at a fixed price for a certain number of years. The price at which this option is provided is called grant price.
Equity SIP	It gives investor an option to systematically invest in equities
Euro Clear Model	A recently introduced settlement platform for government bonds
Exchange Traded Fund (ETF)	A security that tracks an index, a commodity or a basket of assets like an index fund, but trades like a stock on an exchange.
Fiscal Deficit	Excess of Govt. spending over its income, it is generally believed that the countries running large fiscal deficits experience slow economic growth in the medium and long term.
Fundamental Analysis	Systematic study of company fundamentals to arrive at investment decisions
Green Field	Means setting up of new business

Terminology	Description
ITP	Institutional Trading Platform
MUDRA	Micro Units Development Refinance Agency – It is an agency to provide credit at reasonable interest rates to small business units.
OAR	Open Auction Route (bids are invited and the highest bidder(s) get shares. Here parent company can also bid for shares but has to compete with other investors)
P-Note (Participatory Note)	Participatory notes (P-Notes or PNs) are instruments issued by registered foreign institutional investors (FIIs) to overseas investors who wish to invest in Indian Stock Markets without registering themselves with SEBI.
Ponzi schemes (Fraudulent schemes)	A common name given to a fraudulent financial scheme. The name is derived from a scheme developed by Charles Ponzi in the 1920s. A typical Ponzi scheme involves the operator collecting a large amount of money from investors and paying them returns from their own money or the money collected from subsequent investors rather than the profit earned by the person or entity operating such a scheme. Charles Ponzi became notorious for deploying this fraudulent technique while promising 50% return on investment in 45 days and 100% in 90 days.
SBT	Screen based trading done by stock exchange participants. The trading mechanism is all computerized and is done through trading software.
SEC	Security and Exchange Commission (US market regulator like SEBI in India)
SLBS	Security Lending and Borrowing Scheme
Speculator	The speculator is a person who is buying or selling securities for making a quick profit in the near future. He/she is typically interested in forecasting future prices of assets to make a profit.

Terminology	Description
Spot Price	It is cash price share traded at the time in the cash market segment of the NSE (National Stock Exchange)
Stagflation	It is a situation where growth is stagnant while inflation and unemployment are high.
Swing Trading	An investor / speculator who involves in short term buy-sell decisions taking into advantage short term price moves of a security
Technical Analysis	Systematic analysis of stock charts and applying mathematical algorithms to predict stock trends and arriving at investment decisions.
Unit Cost Averaging	Unit cost averaging is a method of timing purchases to reduce the exposure to fluctuations in the price of the security being purchased. An investor using cost averaging splits a purchase of a security into several tranches which are bought at different times. This has the benefit of smoothing out the effects of short term fluctuations in the share price. The price that is finally paid will tend to be closer to the bottom end of the range in which purchases were made than to the top end during a downtrend. To see the reason for this consider a simple example. An investor spends Rs.20,000 buying shares in two tranches of Rs.10,000. The first purchase of 1,000 shares at Rs.10. The price then falls and the next purchase is of 2,000 shares at Rs.5. The average price paid is Rs.20,000 ÷ 3,000 = Rs.6.7. This is less than the average of Rs.10 and Rs.5.

APPENDIX III

Resources

Following are a few resources that are available free of cost on the internet where you can study various aspects of stock markets.

1. **Moneycontrol** – www.moneycontrol.com
2. **Edelweiss** – https://www.edelweiss.in
3. **Equity Master** – https://www.equitymaster.com
4. **Traders Cockpit** – http://www.traderscockpit.com
5. **Technical Analysis** – Stock Charts - http://stockcharts.com/school/doku.php?id=chart_school
6. **India Info Line** – www.indiainfoline.com
7. **Basics of Finance** – https://www.khanacademy.org/economics-finance-domain
8. **Options Market** – http://www.theoptionsguide.com
9. **The Business Line** – http://www.thehindubusinessline.com

10. **Investopedia** – http://www.investopedia.com
11. **Wikipedia (English)** – https://en.wikipedia.org/wiki/Main_Page
12. **TV Channels** – NDTV Profit and CNBC TV18
13. **Jago Investor** – http://www.jagoinvestor.com